W9-BYR-634

TABLE OF CONTENTS

INTRODUCTION

A COMMON-SENSE APPROACH TO PLANT FIRST AID

BETH HANSON

GARDENING OFFERS ITS PRACTITIONERS innumerable intellectual and sensual pleasures—as well as the occasional deep disappointment. One of the most dispiriting discoveries is to find your garden suddenly infiltrated by a mysterious blight. The plants that you started from seed back in March and nurtured through the transition to the outdoors have wilted and collapsed. A prized perennial is drooping and yellow. Circles of seared-looking grass are expanding on your lawn. In many cases, the number of possible causes for a plant's decline can be bewildering: insect damage, nutrient-poor soil, environmental stress, soilborne disease, and disease spread by insect vectors are just a few potential culprits. Many a gardener has experienced helplessness and confusion in the face of such a thicket of possibilities.

This volume, a companion to BBG's earlier handbook *Natural Insect Control: The Ecological Gardener's Guide to Foiling Pests*, covers many of the most common and most devastating diseases that can arise in gardens across the country. In this book you will find descriptions of dozens of diseases of trees, turfgrasses, vegetables, and ornamentals, written by seasoned diagnosticians at university plant pathology departments throughout the United States. It is designed to help you diagnose plant diseases correctly and treat them effectively using the least toxic methods available today. In some cases you may need to consult a more extensive guide to the treatment of specific plant diseases; several excellent resources that also emphasize least-toxic controls are listed at the end of this book.

Probably the most important message you will find here is that plant diseases are best approached through prevention. Disease will inevitably appear

4

NATURAL DISEASE CONTROL

Beth Hanson—Guest Editor

Above: Side-dressing vegetables with compost helps prevent disease.
Cover: Galls on a juniper shoot due to the fungus *Gymnosporangium* that causes rust.

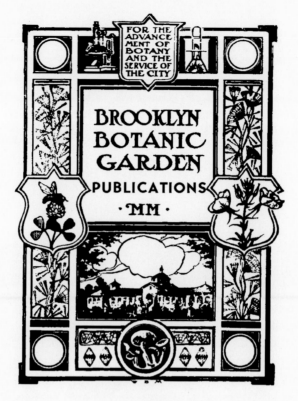

Janet Marinelli
SERIES EDITOR

Sigrun Wolff Saphire
ASSOCIATE EDITOR

Anne Garland
ART DIRECTOR

Steven Clemants
VICE-PRESIDENT SCIENCE & PUBLICATIONS

Judith D. Zuk
PRESIDENT

Elizabeth Scholtz
DIRECTOR EMERITUS

Handbook #164

Copyright © Fall 2000 by the Brooklyn Botanic Garden, Inc.

Handbooks in the *21st-Century Gardening Series,* formerly *Plants & Gardens,*
are published quarterly at 1000 Washington Ave., Brooklyn, NY 11225.

Subscription included in Brooklyn Botanic Garden subscriber membership dues ($35.00 per year).

ISSN # 0362-5850   ISBN # 1-889538-17-5

Printed by Science Press, a division of the Mack Printing Group.

Printed on recycled paper.

Cleaning up the garden in fall and maintaining good sanitation practices year-round keep diseases at bay.

in your garden, but the practices that lead to the overall health of your garden and its many denizens—frequent applications of compost, proper pruning and mowing, wise watering, and good sanitation, among others—can suppress most plant maladies. These same practices will also keep the diseases that do crop up at levels that you can learn to tolerate.

Controlling diseases that get a foothold despite your best efforts may take some experimentation. In the final chapter you will find a thorough discussion of the range of least-toxic controls and the diseases that can be treated with them. You will find out how to mix many of these remedies at home from readily available ingredients, and how to protect yourself and the environment while using them.

As you leaf through these pages, you will familiarize yourself with the symptoms of the most common diseases and pick up pointers on gardening practices that ensure the overall health of your small part of the planet. So the next time disaster strikes, you will have your first aid kit at the ready.

A PLANT DISEASE PRIMER

MIRANDA SMITH

HEALTHY GARDENS TEEM with microorganisms: bacteria, fungi, viruses, virus-like organisms, and nematodes. The majority of these are either benign, coexisting in the soil and on plant surfaces with each other and with the plants around them, or they are beneficial, and perform such tasks as breaking down the compost pile into humus, transforming the nitrogen in the air into forms that plants can use, or preying on pest species. Only a small percentage of microorganisms are pathogenic—that is, capable of causing plant diseases. Fungi are the cause of the largest number of plant diseases, while viruses often cause those with the most severe symptoms. Many pathogens cause only cosmetic or superficial damage. But a few of the most virulent kill their hosts outright and can pose a problem in the garden for years to come.

Plants can also develop disorders. These are not brought on by pathogens, but rather by environmental conditions and stresses. Common examples include blossom end rot of tomatoes and peppers, and tip burn of lettuce, both of which are caused by a calcium deficiency in combination with fluctuating moisture conditions and fluctuating light levels, respectively. In most cases, the symptoms of disorders are confusingly similar to those resulting from pathogenic diseases.

PLANT DEFENSES

Unlike animals, plants don't have an immune system or disease-fighting white blood cells. Instead, they have developed other mechanisms to escape or survive the diseases that attack them. Some plants are simply genetically incompatible with, or immune to, certain diseases. A corn plant can't host tobacco mosaic virus (TMV), a common tomato disease, for example, just as tomatoes can't host the corn disease smut. It is also possible that a particular cultivar, variety, or even an individual plant is immune to a disease that attacks other members of its species, generally

A leaf infected with tomato mosaic virus. Mosaic diseases are characteristic of viruses that interfere with chlorophyll production.

because of subtle differences in the genetic makeup of the various plants.

Resistance to diseases is another factor that protects plants. Although a resistant plant can be susceptible to a particular disease, it is less likely to become infected by it than a non-resistant plant. In some cases, plants are resistant because of a physical characteristic: for example, their cuticles may be too thick for a particular fungus to penetrate, or their stomata, small pores on the leaves, may be closed at the time of day when environmental conditions stimulate disease spores to germinate. Other types of resistance are biochemical: the plant produces enzymes and proteins that inactivate the pathogen.

A plant is described as tolerant to a particular disease if it can be infected by the disease but is unlikely to be killed or severely disabled by it. Tolerance often results from hypersensitivity: a plant may be so sensitive to a disease organism that the cells infected by the pathogen die very rapidly and the disease organism is isolated and cannot move to other areas of the plant tissue.

Plants can also escape infection. Some diseases, such as early blight of tomatoes, primarily attack plants that are young and growing vigorously, while others, such as late blight of tomatoes, attack those that are old and forming more fruit and seeds than new leaves. So plants that are older when early blight strikes have a better chance of surviving, as do those

Infectious diseases are brought on by a fungus, a bacterium, a virus, or nematodes. Clockwise from top left: powdery mildew on lilac leaves; bacterial blight on geranium; rose virus; and foliar nematodes on *Anemone* 'Honorine Jobert'.

that are young when late blight attacks. Similarly, some pathogens, such as many that cause powdery mildew, slowly build to damaging populations as the season progresses, while others, such as *Pythium,* which can cause root rot, are at their most numerous in the early spring. That is to say, it may pay to put off planting crops susceptible to root rot, such as potatoes, until later in spring when the soil has begun to dry, and you may want to take measures to ensure that you can harvest your cucumber crop early, before powdery mildew becomes a problem. When plants do not become infected with a disease simply because of timing, they have "escaped infection."

DISEASE-CAUSING ORGANISMS

BACTERIA
Bacteria cause three types of plant disease symptoms. Some live within a plant's vascular system, the channels through which water and nutrients move from roots to leaves and vice versa. When these organisms become numerous, they are likely to plug up the system, preventing the flow of water and nutrients. Wilts, often beginning on only one side of the plant or even on one branch, are the result.

Other bacteria cause abnormal growth in the cells they have invaded and/or in adjacent cells. These growths, known as galls, may pepper the surface of a leaf or protrude from a stem. They are usually rounded and hard to the touch.

When bacteria kill the cells they infect outright, the results can be rots, internal blights, or spots. Sometimes the spots are small and barely noticeable, but in other cases, cankers, open wounds, or lesions form on bark or soft tissue. When the infection is serious, the bacteria spread and kill the entire leaf, stem, or plant.

Most bacteria are one-celled organisms, although a few are multi-cellular. They reproduce by cell division. Because this reproduction is not sexual, bacteria cannot hybridize. However, that characteristic does not inhibit their ability to evolve; they do exchange genetic information and DNA through plasmid exchange (the exchange of small, DNA-containing elements that exist outside the chromosome), and they mutate relatively easily. Changes in their environment, including ultraviolet light levels and ambient levels of atmospheric gases, as well as subtle changes within their host, can trigger a mutation. This adaptability is responsible for the steadily increasing number of bacteria that cause disease in plants and animals—and the increasing number of bacteria that are immune to antibiotics.

When conditions such as temperature or moisture levels do not suit them, bacteria become dormant. Although many overwinter in the seeds

Wilting can have many causes. It may be due to an infectious disease or be the result of drought stress, as in these squash plants, which have responded to a shortage of water by reducing the surface areas of their leaves to preserve moisture in the heat of day.

of infected plants or inside insects (the pathogen that causes bacterial blight of cucurbits overwinters in the salivary glands of hibernating cucumber beetles, for example), most overwinter on cankers on dormant plants or in the debris of the plant they infected during the growing season. Though a few species can survive for longer than a year in a dormant state, most die after this time. Consequently, rotating crops so they don't grow in the same area again for two to four years is usually an effective control.

FUNGI

Fungi are far more complicated in both structure and reproductive style than bacteria. The fungal body, called a thallus, usually consists of microscopic, threadlike hyphae that spread througout the source of food of the fungus. Collectively, these hyphae are referred to as the mycelium.

The reproductive strategies of different species of fungi vary widely. Some form sclerotia, thickened areas of a hypha, which can break away or overwinter in place and grow into a new organism. Other fungi form spores, tiny bodies that can germinate and grow as seeds do. Some spores are formed asexually; these are usually known as summer spores because they can reproduce as soon as they find appropriate conditions. They tend to die within a few months if they do not find a hospitable environment. Other spores are formed sexually. Many of these are called resting spores because they can remain dormant but viable for months or, if necessary, for many years. Almost all fungal species produce at least two kinds of spores to guarantee their survival, but the fungal rust diseases that require two alternate hosts produce as many as five spore forms over the two years it takes to complete their entire life cycle.

Fungi mutate in the same way that bacteria do; and those that reproduce sexually have the additional advantage of being able to crossbreed. Like bacteria, fungi are capable of evolving rapidly.

Top: a fungus of the genus *Alternaria* infected this tomato plant with early blight, causing lesions on the stem. Bottom: the deformation on this tomato was caused by blossom end rot, a disorder brought on by calcium deficiency in combination with fluctuating moisture levels. Disorders and pathogenic diseases often show very similar symptoms, making diagnosis difficult.

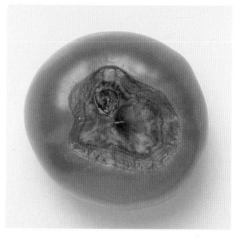

Pathogenic, or disease-causing, fungi produce symptoms that are similar to those caused by bacteria: wilts, galls, rots, spots, cankers, and blights, as well as smuts (large growths filled with spores), scabs (roughened skin tissue), and mildews. These last three symptoms are characterized by the visible presence of the hyphae.

Fungi overwinter in plant debris, seeds, or the soil, as spores or sclerotia. Depending on the species, resting spores can remain viable for two to 20 years. It pays to do some research before simply assuming that a crop rotation will protect your plants from infection by a fungus.

VIRUSES

Viruses that attack plants are just as insidious as those that attack animals. Their physical structure is simple: just a bit of DNA or RNA and a protein covering. Rather than reproducing themselves, viruses stimulate the cell within which they are living to create more viruses. They too evolve quickly in response to changes in their environment.

Viral diseases cause malformations, stunting, and disruption or death of cells containing chlorophyll, which often results in the yellowing of plants (chlorosis). The malformations range from simple leaf curling or puckering to abnormal production of stems or branches, as in the disease called witches' broom. Stunting can be generalized, involving the whole

Colorful yellow spots with orange borders, as on these crabapple leaves, are typical symptoms of *Gymnosporangium* rust, a fungal disease that requires two hosts.

plant, or specific to a particular area. Mosaic diseases are characteristic of viruses that interfere with chlorophyll production. Mosaic-infected leaves are usually mottled with irregularly shaped yellow patches.

Viruses can remain in the host without being active. Many have a fairly narrow band of temperature preference; they are active between 55°F. and 85°F. but not at temperatures above or below this. This characteristic often gives gardeners the false impression that their plants suddenly "got well" from a viral disease.

Plant debris, soils, and gardeners' tools, hands, and shoes can all transport dormant viruses from one host to the next. But viruses remain viable for so long—up to 50 years in some cases—that it is impossible to know for certain how a virus got into a planting. They can also survive the hottest temperatures a compost pile can achieve.

NEMATODES

Nematodes are microscopic animals that look like slender, nonsegmented worms. There are thousands of nematode species, but only a few hundred of them cause plant diseases. These are directly responsible for a number of symptoms, including rotting tissues and abnormal growth, but they also cause diseases indirectly. They can carry viruses, injecting them into the plant as they feed. Moreover, when nematodes pierce the plant tissue to move into cells, secondary pathogenic organisms very often take advantage of the openings to invade the plant.

Nematodes reproduce both sexually and parthenogenetically—that is to say, without the benefit of males. They produce eggs, which are released into the soil around a plant or inside the plant itself. Eggs develop into juveniles, the stage at which most nematodes infect plants; juveniles can also remain dormant but viable for months without a host. Nematodes overwinter in soil or plant tissue as eggs, juveniles, or adults. Egg-to-egg life cycles usually range from three weeks to three months.

SPREADING DISEASE

Pathogens move from host to host in a number of ways. When not seed-borne, bacteria are usually carried by animals, insects, moving water, air currents, and infected soil, or spread around the garden on tools and shoes. Bacteria move into plants through natural openings, such as stomata, or through small wounds and bruises. Once inside a susceptible, living host, their environmental needs are met.

Bacteria reproduce within a host for as long as it continues to feed them. If the bacteria are feeding on the surface of a plant or kill enough cells so that the plant tissue breaks open, they are easily moved from one host to another by wind, falling rain, insects, or even gardeners. Those that feed internally usually overwinter on the plant debris or in the soil, ready to be carried to a new host the following spring.

Fungal spores travel the same routes from host to host as bacteria, but differ in that a spore must germinate and grow before it can infect a plant. Germination is primarily dependent upon temperature and humidity levels. Most fungal species require moderate (50°F. to 90°F.) temperatures and very high humidity or a film of water on the leaves. After germination, most hyphae grow and find their way into a plant through natural openings, wounds, and bruises, but some species have an even more direct route. They form a penetration peg, a toughened tip on the end of the first hypha, that bores through the plant's cuticle layer and into the tissue. Other species release a toxin that kills plant cells; once surface cells are dead, they move into the plant's interior, always killing cells in advance of their spread.

While some fungi can feed only on dead material, and some can feed only on living plants, many of the plant pathogens can feed on either dead or living material. This enables them to remain active after their host is dead, as long as temperatures are tolerable for them; once the weather warms in spring, they can start feeding on the host again and produce a new crop of summer spores that are ready to infect new plants.

Viruses are usually transmitted by insect or nematode vectors—organisms that carry and transmit a disease—and gardeners' hands and tools. Vectors generally transmit the disease by inserting it into the plant as they are feeding. Gardeners are more likely to infect a plant by touching it with dirty hands. Viruses are so small that they can be moved into wounds and bruises that are invisible to the naked eye. As long as the host is alive and susceptible to them, their environmental needs are met.

Nematodes that infect plants do so in their larval stage. If they are not carried to new hosts by moving water or on shoes or tools, they swim through the soil solution. However, due to their size, even the speediest nematode rarely travels more than a foot away from its birthplace. Again, the only requirement for infection is that a susceptible host is alive.

DIAGNOSING DISEASES

Symptoms of various plant diseases look so similar that it's often difficult to diagnose them correctly. However, there is a common-sense approach. Begin by trying to rule out the possibility that the plant has a disorder or non-infectious disease—an ailment caused strictly by environmental or cultural conditions—rather than a disease caused by a pathogen.

Disorders include such things as hollow heart of beets and broccoli as a consequence of a boron deficiency, cat-face of tomato as a consequence of low light levels, and sunburn of tomato or pepper as a consequence of excessive sunlight directly hitting the fruit, when the leaf canopy is lost due to pruning or disease. See pages 67–75 for information on plant disorders.

In general, disorders are fairly uniform throughout a planting or a particular area: if one plant has the problem, the rest do, too, and usually to about the same degree. Diseases are likely to be less generalized. Due to pathogen movement, they may be widespread in the downwind portion of a planting, or along a path where water runs through the garden, but even then, symptoms will vary somewhat from plant to plant. With close enough observation, you may even be able to chart the movement of the pathogen from one plant to the next.

Once you have decided that the problem is caused by an infectious disease, you'll need to try to identify it before you can develop a plan of action. Even if you are the sort of person who dislikes asking for directions when you're lost on the road, it's wise to ask for help in diagnosing a disease. More often than not, seasoned gardeners in your area have seen the disease and can tell you a few things about it. If this fails, get out disease identification books and start looking for likely suspects. Remember that few texts have enough space to list every single plant that a particular disease attacks, but most list the genera or families that host the disease.

As they feed, cucumber beetles may infect squash with bacterial blight of cucurbits, which overwinters in the salivary glands of the hibernating beetles.

Check visual clues too, preferably with a hand lens. Except in the case of spots or internal blights, visual examination with a 10-power lens usually will tell you if the problem is caused by a fungus, bacterium, virus, or nematode. For example, if lesions on the plant are oozing and slimy, chances are that you're looking at hundreds of thousands of tiny bacteria. A mass of threadlike structures is likely to be the mycelium of a fungus, and dry specks that disperse into the air when you breathe on them are probably spores. Leaves that are curled and puckered or have yellowish patches between the veins are an indication that the plant probably has a virus. If the plant looks sickly but you can't see anything above the ground, dig it up. It may have a root-eating pest such as a cabbage root fly maggot or root aphid, but it could also be hosting nematodes. Galls or knots on the root tissue are the sure symptom.

Finally, take a walk around the edges of your property. Look at weedy areas there and in neighbors' yards. It could be that a weed in the same family as your plant is hosting the same disease. Very often, this kind of clue quickly leads to the culprit: a disease that is unrecognizable on your plant might be easy to identify on a weed.

DIAGNOSING
PLANT PROBLEMS

TO IDENTIFY A PLANT PROBLEM, begin by trying to rule out the possibility that it is a disorder caused by environmental conditions rather than a disease caused by a pathogen. In general, disorders, such as the drought stress on dogwood (**A**, below) are fairly uniform throughout a planting; diseases are likely to be more localized. Once you have decided that the problem is caused by a disease, check for visual clues to the type of pathogen. For example, a mass of threadlike structures, such as those of powdery mildew on rose leaves (**B**, below), indicate the presence of a fungus. Yellowish, often striking patches on leaves or fruit, as seen on zucchini (**C**, below), indicate that the plant probably has a virus. If you see no clues above the ground, check the roots; the cyclamen (**D**, below) suffers from root rot.

For more aids to identifying plant problems, consult the charts that follow. The page numbers in the charts will lead you to the "Encyclopedia of Plant Diseases" and "Encyclopedia of Plant Disorders," where there is detailed information on specific problems.

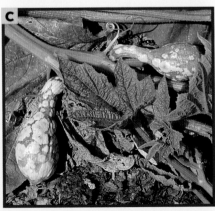

SYMPTOMS &
POSSIBLE CAUSES

ENTIRE PLANT SYMPTOMS

Stunting	Drought stress p. 69, mosaic virus p. 60, salt injury p. 74
Seedlings die	Damping-off p. 30
Orange strings	Dodder p. 31
Wilting	Bacterial wilt p. 56, black root rot p. 26, damping-off p. 30, drought stress p. 69, flooding injury p. 71, *Fusarium* wilt p. 58, *Phytophthora* root rot p. 36, root-knot nematodes p. 61, southern blight p. 41, *Verticillium* wilt p. 62, white mold p. 43

LEAF SYMPTOMS

Wet-looking spots	Anthracnose p. 55, *Botrytis* p. 28, late blight p. 59
Pale spots	Downy mildews p. 32, white smut p. 44
Black spots	Black spot p. 27, *Cercospora* leaf spot p. 29, late blight p. 59, tar spot p. 53
Yellow/orange/red spots (with spores inside)	*Gymnosporangium* rusts p. 51, rose rust p. 39, white pine blister rust p. 54, and many other rusts
Purple/brown spots	Anthracnose of sycamore, ash, and maple p. 45, dogwood anthracnose p. 49, *Entomosporium* leaf spot p. 34, iron/manganese toxicity p. 74, ozone damage p. 68, peony leaf spot p. 35, *Phyllosticta* leaf spot p. 52
Red/brown spots	Bacterial leaf spot p. 26, early blight p. 33, *Volutella* blight p. 42
Olive-green spots	Apple scab p. 45
Tan spots with yellow halo	*Septoria* blight p. 40, bacterial leaf spot p. 26, and other fungal and bacterial diseases
Yellowing or discoloration	Aster yellows p. 24, black root rot p. 26, chlorine injury p. 69, foliar nematodes p. 34, iron deficiency p. 73, mosaic viruses p. 60, nitrogen deficiency p. 74, ozone damage p. 68, peach leaf curl p. 51, *Phytophthora* root rot p. 36, *Pythium* root rot p. 38, root-knot nematodes p. 61, sulfur-dioxide injury p. 68, *Verticillium* wilt p. 62
White/gray/black patches	Downy mildews p. 32, freezing injury p. 71, powdery mildews p. 37, salt injury p. 74, sooty mold p. 75, sulfur-dioxide injury p. 68
Curling or distorting	Azalea leaf gall p. 25, corn smut p. 57, foliar nematodes p. 34, herbicide injury p. 72, mosaic viruses p. 60, peach leaf curl p. 51
Rust-colored bumps	Rose rust p. 39
Leaves drop	Apple scab p. 45
Leaves turn brown or black	Fire blight p. 50

SYMPTOMS & POSSIBLE CAUSES

COMMON PLANTS & THEIR MOST COMMON DISEASES

Diseases marked with an asterisk, though not specifically discussed in the book, are commonly seen. Refer also to the Symptoms chart on pp. 17–18 to help you diagnose a plant problem.

MOST SPRING-BLOOMING PERENNIAL PLANTS
Botrytis gray mold p. 28, root-knot nematodes p. 61, foliar nematodes p. 34
MOST SUMMER-BLOOMING PERENNIALS
Dodder p. 31, root-knot nematodes p. 61, southern blight p. 41
SPRING BULBS
Botrytis gray mold p. 28

Aster ....Aster yellows p. 24, foliar nematodes p. 34, powdery mildews p. 37, root-knot nematodes p. 61, rust*

Chrysanthemum ...Aster yellows p. 24, foliar nematodes p. 34, *Pythium* root rot p. 38, root-knot nematodes p. 61, white mold p. 43

Dahlia ....*Botrytis* gray mold p. 28, foliar nematodes p. 34, root-knot nematodes p. 61, southern blight p. 41, mosaic virus*, white mold p. 43, white smut p. 44

Daisy ....Early blight p. 33, root-knot nematodes p. 61, southern blight p. 41, white mold p. 43

English ivy..............Bacterial leaf spot p. 26

Fern ....Foliar nematodes p. 34

Hardy geranium ....Black root rot p. 26, *Cercospora* leaf spot p. 29, foliar nematodes p. 34

Hosta ....Foliar nematodes p. 34

Hyacinth..............Bacterial leaf spot p. 26

Iris ....Foliar nematodes p. 34, leaf spot*, rust*, southern blight p. 41

Lily ....*Botrytis* gray mold p. 28, foliar nematodes p. 34

Lupine ....*Botrytis* gray mold p. 28, foliar nematodes p. 34, powdery mildews p. 37, root-knot nematodes p. 61, southern blight p. 41

Monarda ....Powdery mildews p. 37, southern blight p. 41

Pachysandra ....Root-knot nematodes p. 61, *Volutella* blight p. 42

Peony ....*Botrytis* gray mold p. 28, foliar nematodes p. 34, leaf spot of peony p. 35, root-knot nematodes p. 61

Phlox..............Foliar nematodes p. 34, powdery mildews p. 37, *Septoria* blight p. 40, mosaic virus*, root-knot nematodes p. 61

Rudbeckia ....Southern blight p. 41

Veronica..............Downy mildews p. 32, root-knot nematodes p. 61, southern blight p. 41

Viola ....Anthracnose p. 55, *Cercospora* leaf spot p. 29, root-knot nematodes p. 61

COMMON PLANTS & THEIR MOST COMMON DISEASES

DECIDUOUS SHRUBS

Amelanchier .... *Entomosporium* leaf spot p. 34, *Gymnosporangium* rusts p. 51

Azalea......................... Azalea leaf gall p. 25, *Cercospora* leaf spot p. 29, dodder p. 31, foliar nematodes p. 34, *Phytophthora* root rot p. 36, root-knot nematodes p. 61, rust*

Brambles .... Anthracnose p. 55, crown gall p. 29, rust*

Cotoneaster .... *Entomosporium* leaf spot p. 34, fire blight p. 50

Currant .... White pine blister rust p. 54

Dogwood................. *Cytospora* canker p. 47, *Septoria* blight p. 40

Euonymus.............. Crown gall p. 29, powdery mildews p. 37

Gooseberry .... White pine blister rust p. 54

Grape .... Anthracnose p. 55, black rot*, crown gall p. 29, powdery mildews p. 37

Lilac....................... Powdery mildews p. 37

Quince .... *Entomosporium* leaf spot p. 34, fire blight p. 50, *Gymnosporangium* rusts p. 51

Rose .... Anthracnose p. 55, black spot p. 27, crown gall p. 29, downy mildews p. 32, powdery mildews p. 37, rose rust p. 39

Viburnum.............. *Cercospora* leaf spot p. 29, downy mildews p. 32

EVERGREEN SHRUBS

Holly...................... Black root rot p. 26, root-knot nematodes p. 61

Inkberry................. Black root rot p. 26

Photinia................. *Entomosporium* leaf spot p. 34

Privet .... Foliar nematodes p. 34

Pyracantha .... Fire blight p. 50, scab*

Rhododendron ...... *Botryosphaeria* canker*, *Phytophthora* root rot p. 36

DECIDUOUS TREES

Almond .... Black knot p. 46, peach leaf curl p. 51

Apple/Crabapple.. Apple scab p. 45, *Cytospora* canker p. 47, fire blight p. 50, *Gymnosporangium* rusts p. 51, powdery mildews p. 37

Apricot.................. Crown gall p. 29, *Cytospora* canker p. 47

Ash .... Anthracnose p. 45

Cherry................... Black knot p. 46, *Cytospora* canker p. 47

Dogwood............... Dogwood anthracnose p. 49, powdery mildews p. 37, *Septoria* blight p. 40

Hawthorn .... Apple scab p. 45, *Entomosporium* leaf spot p. 34, *Gymnosporangium* rusts p. 51

London plane tree.. Powdery mildews p. 37

Maple.................... Anthracnose p. 45, *Cytospora* canker p. 47, *Phyllosticta* leaf spot p. 52, tar spot p. 53

20

DECIDUOUS TREES, CONTINUED

Mountain ash........Apple scab p. 45, *Entomosporium* leaf spot p. 34

Nectarine ....Crown gall p. 29, *Cytospora* canker p. 47, peach leaf curl p. 51

Oak ....Oak leaf blister (*see* peach leaf curl p. 51)

Peach ....Black knot p. 46, crown gall p. 29, *Cytospora* canker p. 47, peach leaf curl p. 51

Pear........................*Cytospora* canker p. 47, *Entomosporium* leaf spot p. 34, fire blight p. 50, *Gymnosporangium* rusts p. 51, pear scab p. 45

Plum ....Black knot p. 46, crown gall p. 29

Poplar ....*Cytospora* canker p. 47

Sycamore................Anthracnose p. 45

Willow....................*Cytospora* canker p. 47

Douglas fir ....*Diplodia* tip blight p. 47

Juniper ....*Gymnosporangium* rusts p. 51, shoot/tip blights p. 41

Pine........................*Diplodia* tip blight p. 47, white pine blister rust p. 54

Spruce....................*Cytospora* canker p. 47, *Diplodia* tip blight p. 47

MOST VEGETABLES

Damping-off p. 30, dodder p. 31, *Pythium* root rot p. 38, root-knot nematodes p. 61, southern blight p. 41

Bean........................Anthracnose p. 55, bacterial wilt p. 56, rust*

Cabbage ....Damping-off p. 30, downy mildews p. 32, *Fusarium* wilt p. 58, root-knot nematodes p. 61, white mold p. 43

Cauliflower............Damping-off p. 30, downy mildews p. 32, root-knot nematodes p. 61, white mold p. 43

Carrot ....Aster yellows p. 24, early blight p. 33, root-knot nematodes p. 61, white mold p. 43

Celery ....Early blight p. 33, *Fusarium* wilt p. 58, root-knot nematodes p. 61, *Septoria* blight p. 40

Corn ....Bacterial wilt p. 56, corn smut p. 57, rust*

Cucumber................Anthracnose p. 55, bacterial wilt p. 56, downy mildews p. 32, gummy stem blight p. 58, mosaic viruses p. 60, powdery mildews p. 37, root-knot nematodes p. 61

Eggplant................Root-knot nematodes p. 61, *Verticillium* wilt p. 62

Lettuce................Downy mildews p. 32, white mold p. 43

COMMON PLANTS & THEIR MOST COMMON DISEASES

VEGETABLES A–Z

VEGETABLES, CONTINUED

Melon..............Bacterial wilt p. 56, *Fusarium* wilt p. 58, gummy stem blight p. 58, powdery mildews p. 37, root-knot nematodes p. 61, southern blight p. 41, white mold p. 43

Onion..............Aster yellows p. 24, dodder p. 31, downy mildews p. 32, root-knot nematodes p. 61, southern blight p. 41, white mold (causes "watery soft rot") p. 43

Parsnip..............Downy mildews p. 32, root-knot nematodes p. 61, white mold (causes "watery soft rot") p. 43

Pea..............*Fusarium* wilt p. 58, southern blight p. 41, mosaic viruses p. 60, white mold p. 43

Pepper..............Early blight p. 33, *Phytophthora* root rot p. 36, root-knot nematodes p. 61, southern blight p. 41, *Verticillium* wilt p. 62, mosaic viruses p. 60, white mold p. 43

Potato..............Aster yellows p. 24, early blight p. 33, *Fusarium* wilt p. 58, late blight p. 59, mosaic viruses p. 60, root-knot nematodes p. 61, *Verticillium* wilt p. 62

Pumpkin..............Downy mildews p. 32, gummy stem blight p. 58, mosaic viruses p. 60

Spinach..............Downy mildews p. 32, *Fusarium* wilt p. 58, white smut p. 44

Squash..............Gummy stem blight p. 58, powdery mildews p. 37

Tomato..............Aster yellows p. 24, bacterial wilt p. 56, early blight p. 33, *Fusarium* wilt p. 58, late blight p. 59, mosaic viruses p. 60, root-knot nematodes p. 61, *Septoria* blight p. 40, southern blight p. 41, *Verticillium* wilt p. 62, white mold p. 43

Turnip..............*Fusarium* wilt p. 58, root-knot nematodes p. 61, white mold p. 43

TURFGRASS

Bentgrass..............Brown patch p. 63, fairy ring p. 64, red thread p. 64, rust p. 65, summer patch p. 66

Annual bluegrass..............Brown patch p. 63, fairy ring p. 64, red thread p. 64, rust p. 65, summer patch p. 66

Fine fescue..............Fairy ring p. 64, red thread p. 64, rust p. 65, summer patch p. 66

Kentucky bluegrass..............Fairy ring p. 64, red thread p. 64, rust p. 65, summer patch p. 66

Ryegrass..............Brown patch p. 63, fairy ring p. 64, red thread p. 64, rust p. 65

Tall fescue..............Brown patch p. 63, fairy ring p. 64, red thread p. 64, rust p. 65

22

ENCYCLOPEDIA OF PLANT DISEASES

S O MANY PLANTS, so many things that may go wrong with them. The following encyclopedia addresses the major infectious diseases that may occur in your garden. Written by regional authorities on plant pathology, the encyclopedia is divided into four main sections: Diseases of Ornamental Plants, Trees, Vegetables, and Turfgrass. Within each section, diseases are organized in alphabetical order. Some diseases, however, attack several types of plants. In that case, you will find the disease listed in each category that it occurs with a cross-reference to the section where it is discussed.

DISEASES OF ORNAMENTAL PLANTS

MARGERY DAUGHTREY, ETHEL M. DUTKY,
WADE H. ELMER, BETH HANSON,
STEPHEN T. NAMETH, MELODIE PUTNAM

ASTER YELLOWS

PLANTS AFFECTED A wide range of annuals, perennials, vegetables, and weeds, including aster, chrysanthemum, cosmos, marigold, petunia, carrot, tomato, onion, and potato
REGIONS AFFECTED Throughout North America
SYMPTOMS Initially, leaf veins lose chlorophyll and turn yellow.

Aster yellows on calendula.

New leaves then yellow and growth becomes bushy and sporadic or stunted. Plants may develop numerous secondary shoots. Flowers may remain green and become distorted. Seeds and fruit fail to develop.

DISEASE CYCLE Aster yellows, a virus-like disease, is caused by a phytoplasma, a single-celled organism that lacks cell walls. This pathogen moves from plant to plant through the feeding of leafhoppers. It overwinters in leafhoppers on perennial host plants. Weeds, including dandelion and plantain, can serve as sources of infection.

PREVENTION AND CONTROL
• Control leafhoppers on lettuce and carrots.
• Screen small plantings with fine-gauge wire mesh to exclude leafhoppers.
• Remove infected plants and discard.
• Control weeds such as dandelion and plantain.
• Seek out resistant varieties.

—BH

AZALEA LEAF GALL

PLANTS AFFECTED Azalea
REGIONS AFFECTED Wherever azaleas are grown
SYMPTOMS This striking disease, caused by the fungus *Exobasidium,* transforms leaves and flowers into swollen, overblown fleshy masses called galls. Expanding flower buds and

Azalea leaf gall.

leaves are most susceptible, and/or a portion of a leaf or flower may be affected. The galls are either greenish or pinkish, eventually becoming white, fading to gray or brown.

DISEASE CYCLE The fungus overwinters in bud scales, and infects young buds as they expand in early spring. The fungus spreads throughout growing leaves and flowers, causing them to swell, and eventually breaks through the gall and sporulates, forming a white, non-powdery surface. Only young tissues are susceptible.

PREVENTION AND CONTROL
• This disease is primarily a cosmetic concern; pick off and destroy the galls before they turn white.
• Do not plant azaleas in heavy shade and avoid wetting the foliage when watering in the spring.
• Disease is most severe when humidity is high in spring or

Bacterial leaf spot on geranium.

when plants are rained on or irrigated from above during the period of leaf expansion.
• Plants in heavy shade and those in areas with poor air circulation are more likely to become diseased.   —*MP*

BACTERIAL LEAF SPOT

PLANTS AFFECTED A variety of garden plants including zinnia, begonia, geranium, hyacinth, and English ivy
REGIONS AFFECTED Throughout the U.S., particularly in areas of warm temperatures and frequent rain or high humidity
SYMPTOMS Bacterial leaf spot is caused by the *Xanthomonas* bacterium. Affected leaves develop reddish to brown, somewhat angular spots, typically surrounded by a yellow halo, which may in turn be surrounded by a water-soaked or greasy-looking halo. Spots tend to appear first on older leaves; however, under conditions of high moisture younger leaves can also show symptoms.
DISEASE CYCLE Plants first show symptoms in the spring, when temperatures become warm (60°F.–80°F.) and leaves remain wet for prolonged periods of time. If moisture and warm temperatures continue, leaf spots will coalesce and cover the entire leaf.
PREVENTION AND CONTROL
• Water early in the morning to allow leaves to dry completely by evening; watering in the evening will only encourage disease development.
• Site plants where they will get plenty of sun and good air movement when mature.
• This disease can be transmitted by seed, particularly in zinnia and begonia; so be sure to purchase clean, bacteria-free seed for the current year's planting.
                                        —*STN*

BLACK ROOT ROT

PLANTS AFFECTED Herbs, annuals, herbaceous perennials, and woody plants including holly and inkberry
REGIONS AFFECTED Throughout North America
SYMPTOMS Yellowing, stunting, wilting in affected plants, along with premature defoliation and dieback of branch tips. Roots of infected plants are black and may feel soft and mushy to the touch. If left unchecked the fungus will

Black root rot.

Black spot on rose leaves.

infect the entire root and eventually lead to plant death.

DISEASE CYCLE Black root rot is caused by the soilborne fungus *Thielaviopsis*, which enters plant roots through root wounds; these are often caused by nematodes. The fungus is more problematic when plants are stressed by overwatering, poor soil, lack of proper nutrition, or high soil pH.

PREVENTION AND CONTROL
• Plant in well-drained soil that contains plenty of organic matter.
• Pay careful attention to proper fertilization, pH, and watering.
• Do not overwater plants, particularly those in heavy soils.
• Discard and compost diseased plants and do not plant susceptible hosts in the affected area for at least two years.   —*STN*

BLACK SPOT OF ROSE

PLANTS AFFECTED Black spot is the most widespread and problematic disease of roses; resistance is rare

REGIONS AFFECTED Throughout the country, although the disease is somewhat less prevalent in arid areas

SYMPTOMS Black spots with irregular, feathery margins form on leaves and may grow to ½ inch wide or merge to form large, dark blotches. Leaves with many spots often yellow and drop. Young stems may also become infected, with spots first appearing as small, raised, purple-red, irregular blotches that become darkened and somewhat blistered.

DISEASE CYCLE *Diplocarpon rosae*, the causal fungus, overwinters on old, spotted leaves and on infected stems. Leaves are infected as they expand in the spring. Leaves must be wet for at least half a day for infection to occur. When infected leaves drop, new leaves may be formed; these can also become infected. Repeated defoliation during a single season can weaken the plant and make it more susceptible to winter injury.

PREVENTION AND CONTROL
• Space plants far enough apart to allow good air circulation, which hastens drying and helps to reduce infection.
• Water from the bottom to avoid sprinkling the leaves.
• Handpick infected leaves as they occur.
• Rake up and remove infected fallen leaves, and prune out affected canes.
• Some resistant rose cultivars are available, but resistance may not hold up in all parts of the country.
• In years of wet spring weather highly susceptible plants can be sprayed with copper fungicides to prevent infection.   —MP

Botrytis gray mold on vinca.

BOTRYTIS GRAY MOLD

PLANTS AFFECTED Gray mold will grow on nearly any plant, but is a particular problem on buds and flowers of ornamentals and vegetables

REGIONS AFFECTED *Botrytis* is universal in distribution, but only causes problems where there is cool weather and continued high humidity or abundant moisture from rain, fog, or irrigation. Arid parts of the country are likely to have fewer problems unless plants are being raised in humid greenhouses or under cover.

SYMPTOMS Flowers or buds first show small, often wet-looking spots, which may stay small or may grow to blight the entire bud or flower. On severely affected plants the fungus can move from the flowers into the leaves and stems, causing leaf blight and stem cankers. Mature or ripening small fruits such as grapes and strawberries may also be affected. In humid weather there will be a fuzzy gray mold on affected tissues.

DISEASE CYCLE Gray mold is a fungal disease caused by various species of *Botrytis*. The fungus overwinters as sclerotia (resistant survival structures) in the soil, as dormant mycelium (the thin, threadlike fungal body) on woody tissues, or as a saprophyte (an organism that feeds on dead plant material on a plant or in the soil). Spores produced in the spring spread by wind or rain splash to succulent new tissue and initiate infections during wet periods.

PREVENTION AND CONTROL

• *Botrytis* is only a problem in damp situations, so managing moisture is the best way to prevent gray mold: do not wet flowers or foliage when watering.

• Prune or space plants for good air circulation so moisture dries rapidly.

• Remove blighted flowers and buds as soon as you observe them.   —*MP*

CERCOSPORA LEAF SPOT

PLANTS AFFECTED A wide variety of plants, including geranium, lobelia, azalea, viola, nasturtium, nicotiana, viburnum, and more

REGIONS AFFECTED Throughout North America

SYMPTOMS Typically, plants develop small black, circular, frog-eye type spots on the older leaves. Other fungi such as *Alternaria* also cause leaf spots in these hosts, but they are much larger (½–¾ inch) than those caused by *Cercospora* (¹⁄₁₆–¼ inch). Spots may coalesce and cause premature leaf drop.

DISEASE CYCLE *Cercospora* leaf spot is caused by the fungus *Cercospora*. It can be particularly problematic in areas of high moisture. The disease first appears in the spring, when over-

Cercospora leaf spot.

wintering fungal spores land on and infect wet leaves.

PREVENTION AND CONTROL

• Water early in the morning so that leaves are completely dry by evening; watering in the evening will only encourage disease development.

• Plant resistant varieties if they are available.

• Plant where there is plenty of sun and good air movement.

• Remove infected plant debris before spring.

• Copper-based fungicides can be an effective control if applied frequently.   —*STN*

CROWN GALL

PLANTS AFFECTED Bramble, stone fruits, rose, grape, nuts, euonymus, and some perennial flowers

REGIONS AFFECTED Throughout North America

SYMPTOMS Aboveground plant

Crown gall.

Damping-off on vinca seedlings.

parts may be stunted and weakened as galls interfere with the movement of water and nutrients through plant. At or around soil line, at the graft union, or on the roots, look for rounded, rough galls up to several inches in diameter. On euonymus, galls can appear anywhere along the stem.

DISEASE CYCLE Crown gall, caused by the soilborne bacterium, *Agrobacterium tumefaciens,* spreads through the soil, in irrigation water, or on tools, entering plants through wounds at the soil line. The bacteria then cause plant cells to proliferate wildly—much as human cancers do—forming growths that swell and darken over time. Bacteria can persist in soil for several years.

PREVENTION AND CONTROL
• Check all new plants for signs of infection; do not accept those with suspicious bumps on roots or stems.

• Avoid wounding stems while cultivating.
• If possible, prune during cold weather, when bacteria are less active.
• Remove and destroy infected plants. Replant with species that are less susceptible to crown gall.   *—BH*

DAMPING-OFF

PLANTS AFFECTED Vegetables, herbs, flowers, and landscape plants
REGIONS AFFECTED Damping-off is widespread and occurs just about anywhere plants are grown. It is more severe where the soils are moist (nearly saturated) and where conditions do not favor rapid growth of seedlings.
SYMPTOMS Seedling stems develop a watery lesion that rapidly dries out; affected tissues then collapse so that the stem looks

pinched together and the plant tips over.

DISEASE CYCLE Damping-off is caused by many species of the widespread soilborne fungi *Fusarium, Pythium* and *Rhizoctonia solani,* which can even attack germinating seeds while still under the soil. (This is called pre-emergent damping-off.) The fungi penetrate germinating seeds and seedlings, causing discoloration and decay of young roots and stems. Rows of seedlings will have gaps where plants did not emerge. Seedlings can also be attacked at or near the soil line shortly after they rise from the ground.

PREVENTION AND CONTROL
• When starting seeds indoors, use sterilized or pasteurized soil mixes and new pots.
• When planting outside, wait until weather is warm and dry enough for rapid germination.
• Avoid overwatering.
• Seeds treated with a biocontrol product containing the fungus *Trichoderma harzianum* (sold as Root Shield) or the bacteria *Bacillus subtilis* (Kodiak) or *Streptomyces griseoviridis* (Mycostop) will be somewhat protected from infection. *—MP*

DODDER

PLANTS AFFECTED Shrubs, perennials, annuals, sometimes vegetables
REGIONS AFFECTED Throughout

North America, especially where clover and alfalfa—two favorite hosts—are grown

SYMPTOMS Stunting, pallor, and eventual death of host plants; mats of stringy orange stems covering large areas of plantings. Center of mass may have black area where host plants have died.

DISEASE CYCLE Dodder is caused by parasitic plants of the genus *Cuscuta,* which cannot produce chlorophyll and depend on host plants for food and water. Dodder seeds are transported in mulch, humus, compost, and soil. They germinate to produce a slender yellow thread that twines around host plants and puts out suckers

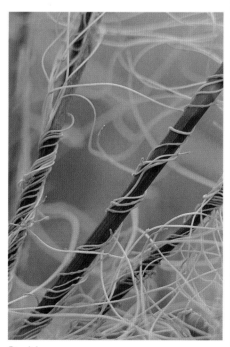

Dodder.

Downy mildew of rose.

called haustoria, which penetrate hosts, eventually forming a tangled mass over large areas. In early summer look for dense clusters of white or pinkish blooms, which can ripen as many as 3,000 seeds per plant by late summer.

PREVENTION AND CONTROL
• In dodder-infested areas, clean tools well after use, wiping off seeds and strands.
• Burn dodder and all infested plant parts before dodder seeds ripen.
• Examine new planting areas closely for dodder; hoe lightly and repeatedly to allow dodder seed to germinate and die before planting.   —*BH*

DOWNY MILDEWS

PLANTS AFFECTED Cabbage, cauliflower, cucumber and other cucurbits, hardy geranium, grape, lettuce, nicotiana, onion, rose, snapdragon, spinach, strawflower, veronica, viburnum, and others

REGIONS AFFECTED Downy mildew fungi are most active in cool-temperature climates (generally 45°F.–65°F.) with extended periods of high humidity

SYMPTOMS Often pale or brown spots on the upper surfaces of leaves, but most characteristic is the outgrowth of downy patches of light gray, violet, or whitish sporulation (production of spores) on the leaf underside during periods of high humidity. On roses, downy mildew can look like spray injury and will cause defoliation. Outbreaks often are noted during spring and fall in the northern U.S.; the disease is much less active during hot, dry summer periods.

DISEASE CYCLE There are many different downy mildew fungi, including different species of *Basidiophora, Bremia, Peronospora, Pseudoperonospora,* and *Sclerospora.* Fungi produce sporangia (a type of spore structure) on stalks that grow out of the stomata, or small openings, in the undersides of infected leaves; these are disseminated by wind-driven rain or by insects. The fungi usually survive the winter as oospores (thick-walled spores resulting from sexual reproduction and resistant to temperature and moisture stress) that form inside infected leaves. These contaminate the soil where a diseased plant has grown.

PREVENTION AND CONTROL
• Inspect transplants for symptoms.
• Space plants wide enough apart to allow for good air circulation.
• Water early in the day, and avoid wetting the foliage.
• Water thoroughly and avoid frequent, light waterings.
• Remove individual infected leaves or plants as soon as symptoms appear.
• Collect and dispose of plant debris in the fall (do not compost).
• Crop rotation will help to avoid infection via the soil.   *—MD*

EARLY BLIGHT

PLANTS AFFECTED A wide variety of garden plants including celery, carrot, tomato, pepper, potato, daisy, zinnia, and impatiens; many species of the causal fungus *Alternaria* are specific to their host plants and will not infect other plants
REGIONS AFFECTED Wherever host plants are grown
SYMPTOMS Older leaves first develop circular, brown or black target-like spots with irregular yellowish halos; these spots develop concentric rings. Fruit and stem infections are similar but usually not numerous.
DISEASE CYCLE The fungus *Alternaria* can be seedborne and can overwinter on plant residues.

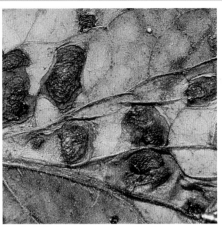
Early blight on tomato leaf.

Alternaria often attacks seedlings in cold frames during periods of overcast skies and cool weather. Wet weather and high humidity are conducive to disease outbreaks. Lesions will sporulate, producing additional spores, which are spread onto new tissues by wind-driven rains. The dead colonized tissue provides the overwintering spores that will cause the disease in the spring.
PREVENTION AND CONTROL
• Sanitation can reduce overwintering inoculum: remove or bury affected garden plant refuse.
• Space plants properly to ensure good ventilation.
• Irrigate in the morning to allow time for leaves to dry.
• Resistant varieties exist for some species.
• Several copper-based fungicides are available; consult label for dosage rates and safety precautions.   *—WHE*

ENTOMOSPORIUM LEAF SPOT

PLANTS AFFECTED Photinia, pear, English hawthorn. Quince, *Amelanchier*, mountain ash, and cotoneaster may also be affected.
REGIONS AFFECTED Photinia leaf spot caused by the fungus *Entomosporium* is nearly universal, occurring wherever photinia is grown. Hawthorns can be affected by *Entomosporium* in most areas except the arid South, whereas pears are primarily affected in the eastern U.S.
SYMPTOMS The fungus *Entomosporium* causes leaf spot and blight. Spots start out small, purple, and round. Spots are rarely larger than ¼-inch in diameter, but leaves may become covered with spots that coalesce. Heavily spotted leaves may turn yellow and drop. Defoliation may be extensive in heavily affected plants, weakening them. Twigs may become diseased as well, with small purple or black lesions appearing on the current year's growth.
DISEASE CYCLE For all hosts, areas with extended cool, wet weather during late spring and early summer will have problems with *Entomosporium* leaf spots. Disease will be worse on plants growing in the shade or in areas with poor air circulation. The fungus overwinters on twigs and in leaf spots. Spores produced in the spring initiate new infections. Spores are spread via wind and rain splash.
PREVENTION AND CONTROL
• When selecting trees for new plantings, choose those with resistance.
• Avoid wetting the foliage when watering.
• Rake and dispose of leaves and prune out and destroy blighted twigs.
• Control on existing, highly susceptible plants may be difficult without applications of copper-based fungicides.   *—MP*

Entomosporium leaf spot.

FOLIAR NEMATODES

PLANTS AFFECTED Almost all garden plants, including ferns, lilies, hosta, peony, and some woody plants such as azalea and privet
REGIONS AFFECTED Woodland habitats throughout the temperate regions of the world, and

greenhouses and nurseries

SYMPTOMS By midsummer, subtle discolored areas may be visible on infected foliage. These areas resemble patchwork, as they are clearly bounded by leaf veins; nematodes cannot move across major leaf veins. In monocots such as hosta, lily, and iris, discoloration appears as streaks bounded by the parallel veins. Eventually infected leaves turn brown or black and die.

DISEASE CYCLE Most plant parasitic nematodes live in the soil and feed on roots; a few species, including the foliar nematode, feed in the stems and foliage causing distortions, discoloration, and death of foliage. In fall, the nematodes migrate down the plant and overwinter in the buds and crown; they can remain alive in dry leaf tissue for many years. In spring, the nematodes crawl up the plant and enter the leaf through the stomata, small pores on the underside of the leaf. A film of water on plant surfaces is required for the nematode to move around on the plant. Once inside the leaf, the nematode will grow and reproduce. For most of the growing season, the nematodes feed inside the leaf and reproduce, attaining large populations by late summer.

PREVENTION AND CONTROL
• In temperate areas, foliar nematodes are mainly a cosmetic

Foliar nematodes on geranium.

problem because little harm is done by the time symptoms appear late in the growing season.
• Avoid introducing foliar nematodes into the garden. Buy plants late in the season, so you will see the symptoms if the plants are infected.   *—EMD*

LEAF SPOT OF PEONY

PLANTS AFFECTED Peonies
REGIONS AFFECTED Areas with summer rains or high humidity; the disease is usually not present in more arid areas of the country or in areas where summer rains fall infrequently
SYMPTOMS Peonies are subject to a number of fungal leaf spots that usually appear late in the growing season. Symptoms usually start out as small, round discolored areas (brown or purplish) that run together to form irregular blotches. Entire

Leaf spot of peony.

Phytophthora root rot.

leaves can then be blighted, turning brown and dying. These diseases often show up at the end of the season, when they cause relatively little damage. In years with heavy rains or abundant humidity these leaf spots can show up earlier in the year and cause more substantial damage.

DISEASE CYCLE Leaf spots are caused by various fungi that overwinter on peony plant debris. Spores produced in the spring initiate new infections.

PREVENTION AND CONTROL
• Prune affected plants to the ground and destroy the debris.
• Move plants from dense shade or areas with poor soil drainage and poor air circulation to more appropriate locations.
• Water plants from the bottom to keep moisture off the leaves and avoid excessive irrigation.
—*MP*

PHYTOPHTHORA ROOT ROT

PLANTS AFFECTED
Rhododendron, azalea, and other woody ornamentals

REGIONS AFFECTED Areas of North America where soils are heavy or have a non-acidic pH, or in areas of heavy rainfall (East, Midwest, and Pacific Northwest)

SYMPTOMS Initially, foliage will become dull as root health declines; leaves may turn yellow and wilt. These changes may take place quickly or over several months. Infection may occur on part of the root system, so leaf and stem symptoms may appear on one side of the plant. Rotted roots will be brown and mushy, and you may be able to easily slide outer root tissue off the inner root core, which will look like a tiny piece of white or brown thread. Woody perennials may live in a state of reduced vigor and decline for years.

DISEASE CYCLE *Phytophthora* root rot of woody ornamentals is caused by the soilborne fungus *Phytophthora*. Spores infect root tips when soils are saturated with water for extended periods. Once inside the root, the fungus produces enzymes that break down root cells, eventually leading to root death. The fungus then grows up the root to the crown of the plant and causes rot.

PREVENTION AND CONTROL

• Make sure that the soil at the planting site drains well, or plant in a raised bed.

• Plant at the proper depth and do not mulch too high up the plant crown.

• If disease appears, change cultural practices to increase plant vigor; for example, use a fertilizer that promotes acidic conditions.

• Acidic soils inhibit disease development. Add organic matter such as peat or compost to soils.

—STN

POWDERY MILDEWS

PLANTS AFFECTED African violet, apple, aster, deciduous azalea, begonia, crabapple, dogwood, lilac, London plane tree, lupine, *Monarda*, phlox, poinsettia, rose, squash, and others. Each host is infected by a specific powdery mildew fungus.

REGIONS AFFECTED Wherever host plants are grown

SYMPTOMS The characteristic symptom is the fungus itself: white, granular-looking colonies roughly ¼-inch in diameter on the upper and lower leaf surface. Infection can also occur on stems, flowers, and fruits. In some cases, infection will cause stunting or curling of the young, developing leaves. Usually the injury is merely aesthetic. In some instances, visible fungus is very sparse, and infected tissue may be red, purplish, or black.

DISEASE CYCLE During the growing season, and all year long in greenhouses, fungi produce copious numbers of spores (causing a distinctive "granular sugar" texture). Spores move on air cur-

Powdery mildew on *Monarda*.

rents from plant to plant. In temperate climates, the fungus overwinters in the vegetative buds of a woody perennial host, or produces specialized protective spore cases called cleistothecia. To the naked eye, these appear as a peppering of small black dots on the surface of infected plant parts in autumn. The spores inside the cleistothecia are released in the spring, when new plant growth is available for infection. Unlike most other fungal diseases, powdery mildews are not favored by extended periods of leaf wetness. In the northern parts of the U.S., they are diseases of summer and fall rather than spring. Powdery

mildews on lilacs and asters, for example, become especially evident in late summer, when these diseases are favored by high humidity and natural temperature fluctuations.

PREVENTION AND CONTROL
• Seek out cultivars that are less susceptible.
• Plant in sunny locations with adequate spacing between plants to allow good air movement.
• Irrigate thoroughly when needed, rather than providing frequent light waterings.
• Locate mildew-prone plants where their foliage will be obscured by plants with eye-catching displays of flowers or fruit in late summer and fall.
• Potassium bicarbonate fungicides and horticultural-oil sprays are effective against powdery mildews. Use cautiously, however, as excessive application of either of these can injure plants.
—*MD*

PYTHIUM ROOT ROT

PLANTS AFFECTED Woody and non-woody plants and cuttings of these, bedding plants, vegetables, herbs, and many other plants
REGIONS AFFECTED In greenhouse-grown plants or potted houseplants, and outdoors in wet soils
SYMPTOMS Initially, an overall yellowing of the foliage or browning of the edges of the leaves;

Pythium root rot (left).

wilting and stunting may also occur. Roots will be discolored, soft, and watery. With advanced decay, the outer portion of the root may slough off, leaving only a thin, stringy central core (called a rat-tail). *Pythium* can also attack rooted cuttings, where it causes blackening of the cut end and decay of the roots.

DISEASE CYCLE Several members of the fungal genus *Pythium* can cause rot of the fine "feeder" roots of many plants. *Pythium* is a soilborne fungus that is present in most soils. Very wet soils encourage the fungus to produce spores. These move in soil water to plant roots, germinate, enter roots, and grow through tissues, eventually producing resting spores that overwinter in plant debris. The overwintering spores then germinate and infect plant roots directly or produce the spores that move in soil water.

PREVENTION AND CONTROL
• Use sterilized or pasteurized soil mixes and new pots for propagating and growing plants.
• Use a suppressive soil medium such as composted pine, fir, or hardwood bark for plants in pots or in planter boxes.
• Do not over-fertilize or let plants dry out.
• Avoid overwatering.
• Remove and destroy any symptomatic plants.
• Treat plants with biocontrol products containing the fungus *Trichoderma harzianum* (sold as

Rose rust.

Root Shield) or the bacteria *Bacillus subtilis* (Kodiak) or *Streptomyces griseoviridis* (Mycostop); these will help prevent infection, but must be applied before there is any sign of disease. *—MP*

ROSE RUST

PLANTS AFFECTED Primarily Hybrid Tea and Floribunda roses; most shrub and antique roses are less susceptible

REGIONS AFFECTED Wherever roses are grown, particularly in the East, Midwest, and Pacific Northwest, where leaf moisture is common; the disease is not as severe in drier climates

SYMPTOMS Orange- or rust-colored growth on the undersides of leaves; upper surfaces may have yellow or brown spots. Older leaves tend to show symptoms first. Under favorable conditions of cool temperatures and high

Septoria blight.

moisture, rust can cover the entire leaf and stem of the rose plant.

DISEASE CYCLE Rose rust is caused by the fungus *Phragmidium*. When leaf surfaces are moist, the fungus can infect hosts via airborne spores, or via fungal hyphae in cane cankers in milder climates. Severe infections can cause stem and leaf deformation and premature leaf loss. If defoliation persists over a period of years, infected plants may die.

PREVENTION AND CONTROL
• Plant resistant varieties, shrub, or antique-type roses.
• Water early in the day so that leaves can dry out by the evening: leaves that are wet overnight are susceptible to infection.
• Plant roses in areas that have full sun and allow air to flow freely around the plants.
• Clean up and compost infected

leaf debris and prune out dead cankers prior to spring.   —*MP*

SEPTORIA BLIGHT

PLANTS AFFECTED Tomato, celery, dogwood, and phlox; the disease can also occur on eggplant, but does not cause damage
REGIONS AFFECTED Wherever host plants are grown, but environmental conditions must be conducive for the disease to develop
SYMPTOMS Older leaves initially develop small necrotic (dead) spots that enlarge and develop a chlorotic (yellowish) halo. Lesions can coalesce and eventually cause the leaf to drop off.
DISEASE CYCLE *Septoria* blight is caused by species in the genus *Septoria*. The fungus overwinters on plant residues in fungal structures called pycnidia. Warm rains cause these structures to swell and release their spores on leaves. The disease is favored by warm, wet conditions during periods of overcast skies. Lesions sporulate, producing additional spores, which are spread onto new tissue by wind-driven rains. The disease may not appear until mid- to late season. Diseased tissue colonized by the fungus provides the overwintering inoculum (pathogen tissue responsible for causing infection).

PREVENTION AND CONTROL
• Sanitation is important to reduce overwintering inoculum: discard or deeply bury last year's garden residues.
• Proper plant spacing ensures good ventilation.
• Avoid overhead irrigation and/or irrigate in the morning to allow time for leaves to dry.   —*WHE*

SHOOT/TIP BLIGHTS ON JUNIPERS

PLANTS AFFECTED Many species of juniper, especially creeping junipers
REGIONS AFFECTED The normal range of junipers—most of the U.S.; it is not a problem in tropical, desert, and arctic regions
SYMPTOMS On junipers affected by *Phomopsis* shoot blight, infected shoots turn pale green in spring, then brown. Shoots infected by *Kabatina* tip blight turn brown by late winter, and have a small, ashy gray canker at the base.
DISEASE CYCLE The fungus *Phomopsis juniperovora* infects tender new growth in the spring, and infected shoots die by early summer. The fungus *Kabatina juniperi* attacks shoots in warm summer weather and into the fall, invading through tiny wounds and killing shoots. Both diseases produce small, dark pinpoint fungal fruiting bodies in dead shoots, from which microscopic spores are released to cause new infections. Moist weather is required for infection.
PREVENTION AND CONTROL
• Plant resistant species or cultivars; when symptoms are severe, replace infected plants with a resistant variety.
• Some popular juniper varieties are so susceptible to *Kabatina* blight that they should not be grown in affected areas. These include: *Juniperus chinensis* 'Kaizuka', 'Spartan'; *J. horizontalis*, 'Bar Harbor', 'Blue Horizon', 'Emerson Creeper', 'Plumosa Compacta', 'Wiltoni'; *J. scopulorum* 'Sky Rocket'; and *J. virginiana*, 'Nova'.   —*EMD*

SOUTHERN BLIGHT

PLANTS AFFECTED A large number of vegetables, herbaceous ornamentals, and some woody plants
REGIONS AFFECTED As its name

Southern blight.

suggests, this disease occurs in the southern half of the U.S.
SYMPTOMS This disease is easily identified by the white fluffy threads of the fungus that spread up the stem and across the soil. It also produces small, nearly perfectly round fungal bodies (sclerotia) in infected tissue; these look similar in size and shape to mustard seeds. Other symptoms include stem cankers, wilt, yellowing, blight of the whole plant, and rot of bulbs, fleshy roots, and tubers.
DISEASE CYCLE The disease is caused by the soilborne fungus *Sclerotium rolfsii*, which resides in the soil and in infected plant residue. It usually attacks the plant at the stem near the soil line, forming white tufts of the fungus that move up the stem. The disease is worst in warm, moist, sandy soils, especially those low in nitrogen.

Volutella blight.

PREVENTION AND CONTROL
• Remove and destroy any affected plants.
• Remove the surrounding soil (to 6 inches below and beyond the root system) and replace with soil from an uninfected area.
• Bury all plant residues so that the fungus will not remain on the soil surface.
• Increase organic content of soil, for example by adding mature compost.
• Vegetables can be protected with a strip of aluminum foil that is loosely wrapped around the stem and buried a couple of inches below the soil. This creates a physical barrier so the fungus cannot reach the stem.
• Solarize soil.　　　　—MP

VERTICILLIUM WILT

PLANTS AFFECTED Sunflower, several herbs.
See Diseases of Vegetables, p. 62

VOLUTELLA BLIGHT OF PACHYSANDRA

PLANTS AFFECTED All varieties of *Pachysandra*
REGIONS AFFECTED Throughout North America
SYMPTOMS Leaves of infected plants first develop brown, target-like blotches, often on areas previously damaged by stresses such as sun scorch; these later become generally blighted. Stem cankers and blackish discol-

oration will develop and cause a dieback of the plants. Cankers may appear anywhere on the stem. Circular, spreading areas of diseased plants will be noticeable in the planting.

DISEASE CYCLE When conditions are moist for extended periods, orangish pink spore masses of the *Volutella* fungus may develop. The disease spreads via airborne spores or through spores in splashing water. The disease is especially severe when plants are crowded, humidity is high, and weather is wet.

PREVENTION AND CONTROL
• Always select and plant high-quality plant material. Choose plants that are growing well, are dark green in color, and appear to be free of nutritional deficiencies (yellowing).
• In established beds, remove infected plants and prune out diseased parts of plants.
• Thin planting to remove dense growth in fall, during dry weather.
• Fertilize appropriately to maintain plant vigor.
• Avoid overhead watering and water early in the day so that drying occurs before evening. —*STN*

WHITE MOLD

PLANTS AFFECTED Annual bedding plants, herbaceous perennials, and vegetables
REGIONS AFFECTED Throughout North America
SYMPTOMS Plants wilt and develop a small, cotton ball-like growth at the base of the stem. When disease is in the late stages, the whole plant may collapse to the ground and rot. Host plants with pithy stems may contain the black, hard, overwintering structure of the cottony rot fungus.

DISEASE CYCLE White mold disease is caused by the soilborne *Sclerotinia* fungus. Airborne fungal spores infect flowers; soilborne fungal hyphae (branching filaments) penetrate host plants at the soil level. Once inside the host, the pathogen produces cell-degrading enzymes that cause a soft

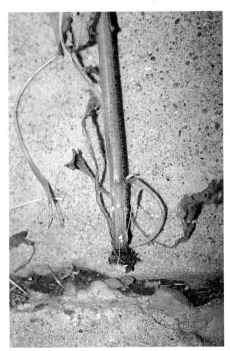

White mold.

White smut.

rot of the tissue. Plants are most susceptible during flowering or during periods of frequent rains.

PREVENTION AND CONTROL
• The overwintering structure is highly adaptable to extreme environmental conditions, so avoid transporting infected soil and plant material.
• Remove infected plants from the garden and destroy or dispose of them. Do not compost.
• Plant a non-host in the affected area; this may eliminate the disease.
• Solarize soil.   *—STN*

WHITE SMUT

PLANTS AFFECTED Most commonly dahlia, calendula, cosmos, spinach, and *Gaillardia*
REGIONS AFFECTED Wherever host plants are grown
SYMPTOMS The fungus grows and forms spores within the leaf tissue, causing pale (white or yellow) round leaf spots, which later turn brown. On dahlia, the spots can be as much as ½-inch in diameter; on cosmos, white patches resembling powdery mildew form on the threadlike leaves.

DISEASE CYCLE White smuts are caused by various fungi in the genus *Entyloma;* each has a limited host range. Plants belonging to the same plant family may be affected by the same type of white smut. During the growing season, the fungus can spread when tiny spores called sporidia that coat the upper surface of the leaf spots are splashed around with rain. The dark teliospores formed within the leaf tissue allow the fungus to overwinter within plant debris and cause new infections in the spring. White smuts may be seedborne, or introduced to the garden via infected plants.

PREVENTION AND CONTROL
• Inspect transplants for symptoms before purchasing.
• If symptoms appear, remove affected leaves.
• Irrigate at ground level if possible to minimize splashing and wetting of leaves.
• Change planting locations if white smut has been severe the previous year.
• Hot-water treatment of seed may eliminate white smut contamination.   *—MD*

DISEASES OF TREES

ETHEL M. DUTKY, BETH HANSON,
STEPHEN T. NAMETH, MELODIE PUTNAM,
KAREN L. SNOVER

ANTHRACNOSE

PLANTS AFFECTED Sycamore, maple, and ash
REGIONS AFFECTED Throughout the U.S. in areas where spring temperatures are cool and there is moisture from rain or fog
SYMPTOMS Symptoms vary among tree species. Infected maples develop small to large, somewhat circular, light brown areas of dead leaf tissue along and including the veins, extending to the leaf margins. Ash leaves develop large, irregular, brown areas that tend to follow the veins to the margin. On sycamore, bud and twig infection can completely kill young leaves and twigs.
DISEASE CYCLE Moisture and temperatures of 50°F.–55°F. just after bud break are critical for infection of new, developing leaves by fungi of the genus *Gnomonia*. Spores produced by fungal mycelium that overwinters in twig cankers are the primary source of spring infection. Ash and sycamore have different bud break times. Depending on the coincidence of cool weather and bud break, anthracnose may be more prevalent on ash one year and sycamore in another.
PREVENTION AND CONTROL Practice good tree care to increase resistance to infection: fertilize, prune, and, during drought, water. If infection is severe, vigorous trees will more quickly produce new leaves to replace blighted ones. Continued defoliation weakens trees and often makes them unsightly, but rarely kills them.   *—STN*

APPLE SCAB

PLANTS AFFECTED Apple, crabapple, mountain ash, hawthorn. Pear scab, caused by the closely related organism, *Venturia pyri-*

Apple scab.

na, can also be managed using the tactics outlined below

REGIONS AFFECTED Wherever apples are grown but less common in hot, dry regions

SYMPTOMS Olive-green spots first appear on leaves and fruit; petioles, pedicels, and twigs can also be affected. As spots age, they become greenish black and velvety. If infection is severe, early defoliation may occur, reducing flower bloom and/or fruit yield the following year. Affected fruits may become deformed and cracked.

DISEASE CYCLE The disease, caused by the fungus *Venturia inaequalis*, is often quite severe when spring is rainy and cool. About the time buds begin to develop, fungal spores are produced on overwintering leaf debris and are splashed by rain and blown by wind onto developing plant tissue, initiating infections. Spots appear on newly formed leaves; inside the spots, more spores are produced that spread infection to other parts of the tree. Again, rainy weather greatly encourages spore spread and infection during the secondary phase of spore production. The fungus overwinters on fallen leaves.

PREVENTION AND CONTROL

• Collect and dispose of fallen leaves in autumn.

• Plant resistant varieties.

• Fruit damage is quite superficial; cut away the scabby area and eat the clean, healthy fruit tissue below.   —*KLS*

BLACK KNOT

PLANTS AFFECTED All *Prunus* species; disease is most severe on plum and cherry

REGIONS AFFECTED Throughout the U.S. and Canada

SYMPTOMS Small, light brown swellings on current or last season's growth often go unnoticed and the disease becomes evident only once they have enlarged into olive-green knots with a velvety texture the following spring. Warty black galls, varying in size from ½ inch to more than 1 foot in length, make an unsightly appearance on infected trees. Knots will continue to grow until they girdle and kill the branch.

DISEASE CYCLE The fungal pathogen, *Apiosporina morbosa*, usually infects young succulent twigs between April and June

during warm, wet weather. The fungal spores are produced on living galls one to several years old.

PREVENTION AND CONTROL

• Prune out all knots during the winter season; destroy or bury pruned branches.

• Plant resistant varieties.

• Fungicide sprays (lime-sulfur may be effective) may be necessary if the disease has been severe in the past, but this should only be considered as a last resort. Eradicating black knot infections on wild *Prunus* species is impossible. Cultivated trees should be monitored and pruned routinely.   —*KLS*

CYTOSPORA CANKER

PLANTS AFFECTED A wide range of woody plants, including stone fruits, apples, pears, spruces, maples, poplars, and willows

REGIONS AFFECTED Throughout U.S., wherever host plants grow

SYMPTOMS Yellowing, wilting, dieback of new shoots; black or reddish discoloration on the bark of infected twigs; gummy cankers on trunks and branches that grow until they girdle the infected part.

DISEASE CYCLE Fungi of the genus *Cytospora* overwinter on infected parts, and are spread by splashing rain, insects, and pruning tools; fungi enter new hosts through wounds and leaf scars. Trees of low vigor are often most susceptible.

Black knot.

PREVENTION AND CONTROL

• Plant resistant cultivars.

• Avoid wounding bark with lawn mower.

• Remove infected parts, pruning during dry weather; disinfect pruners with bleach solution between cuts.

• Contribute to tree vigor by proper fertilizing, but avoid nitrogen-based fertilizers.   —*BH*

DIPLODIA TIP BLIGHT OF PINES

PLANTS AFFECTED Mature Austrian, Scots, and Japanese black pines; also mugo, red, scrub, and Virginia pines;

Diplodia tip blight on Austrian pine.

occasionally spruces and Douglas fir

REGIONS AFFECTED Throughout the temperate U.S.

SYMPTOMS By early summer new growth turns brown and dies. Needles may be stunted, about a third to half of full size. Resin flow from infected (dead) shoots is often conspicuous. After several years, lower branches may develop clubbed tips from repeated blighting of new shoots, and branches eventually die. Look for small, black fungal fruiting structures called pycnidia embedded in dead tissue of needles, twigs, and cones, especially under the sheath at the base of dead needles. Symptoms can be confused with those caused by insect borers. Cut into the dead shoot; a hollow space indicates borer damage. A correct diagnosis is essential to selecting an effective control. This disease is worse on pine species that retain their cones for several years than on species that drop their cones every year.

DISEASE CYCLE *Diplodia* tip blight is caused by the fungus *Sphaeropsis sapinea* (formerly named *Diplodia pinea*). Many microscopic fungal spores are exuded from the pycnidia in wet weather and washed onto susceptible new growth, causing new infections. Wet, rainy weather is required for new infections in spring and early summer. The fungus can infect trees through wounds during the entire growing season, and remains in infected shoots and cones from year to year.

PREVENTION AND CONTROL
• Remove dead branches, cones, and fallen debris. Wait for dry fall weather to prune: the fungus can infect pruning cuts in wet weather conditions.
• Do not plant susceptible pines close to old, infected trees: fungal spores can splash from old trees onto young ones.
• Preserve the vigor of trees by mulching around the base; prevent damage to roots from compaction or digging.
• Water during prolonged drought, but do not use overhead irrigation in spring, as this will promote disease.   —*EMD*

DOGWOOD ANTHRACNOSE

PLANTS AFFECTED All types of dogwoods; flowering dogwood (*Cornus florida*) and Pacific dogwood (*C. nuttallii*) are most susceptible

REGIONS AFFECTED Common in the South, Midwest, East, and Northeast

SYMPTOMS Leaf symptoms include irregular brown blotches bordered in purple on upper leaf surfaces (tan when viewed from the leaf underside). Leaf lesions often are delimited by the leaf midvein in the early stages. Stem symptoms include twig dieback and stem cankering and dieback, often with visible fungal fruiting bodies on dead twigs.

DISEASE CYCLE Caused by the fungus *Discula destructiva*, this disease is most severe where cool, moist conditions occur during the summer, and in densely vegetated, shady sites with poor air movement. Infections occur during moist conditions from the period of early bud break through early leaf development. Airborne fungal spores and fungal hyphae that have overwintered in twig and stem cankers are the primary source of infection. The disease appears to be less prevalent in recent years due to the planting of more resistant varieties.

Dogwood anthracnose.

PREVENTION AND CONTROL
• Plant in sites with good drainage, adequate organic matter, and partial shade (e.g., just morning sun). Provide moderate fertility; mulch to moderate soil temperatures.
• Prune dead branches promptly.
• Use proper fertilization, pruning, watering, and pest control practices to encourage vigorous plant growth.
• Plant resistant varieties if possible; some cultivars of Chinese or Japanese dogwood (*C. kousa*) are somewhat resistant.   —*STN*

DISEASES OF TREES

Fire blight.

ENTOMOSPORIUM LEAF SPOT

PLANTS AFFECTED Pear, English hawthorn, quince, mountain ash. *See* Diseases of Ornamental Plants, p. 34

FIRE BLIGHT

PLANTS AFFECTED Apple, pear, quince, crabapple, cotoneaster, pyracantha, hawthorn, and other members of the Rosaceae (Rose Family).
REGIONS AFFECTED From its native region around New York State, this disease has spread across the U.S. with the cultivation of apples and pears. It is now most severe in the Southeast.
SYMPTOMS First flowers, then fruits brown and shrivel; leaves turn brown or black; both remain attached to twigs. As cankers form, bark shrinks, turning dark brown or purplish; cankers may ooze infectious gum. The disease spreads rapidly on individual trees. It was given the common name fire blight because it moves through an orchard like fire, with the trees looking as if they were torched.
DISEASE CYCLE The bacterium *Erwinia amylovora* spreads from blossom to blossom and plant to plant in spring on insect vectors such as ants, flies, wasps, and bees. Infection spreads to developing fruit, and then down the pedicel (stalk) to leaves. Rain or overhead irrigation splashes bacteria to new sites on plants. Bacteria multiply very rapidly, and can form collars of cankers near base of tree. Bacteria overwinter on cankers.
PREVENTION AND CONTROL
• Grow resistant varieties.
• Prune carefully and frequently, cutting at least 6–8 inches below infected areas; clean tools in a 25-percent bleach solution between cuts. Dispose of pruned parts.
• In spring, use slow-release fertilizers such as aged manure rather than nitrogen-based fertilizers, which encourage the rapid, tender growth preferred by the bacterium.
• If infection is severe, bordeaux

mixture sprayed during bloom can be effective.   —*BH*

GYMNOSPORANGIUM RUSTS

PLANTS AFFECTED Pomaceous plants (apple, hawthorn, pear, quince, *Amelanchier*, and others) and cedars (*Juniperus* species)
REGIONS AFFECTED Wherever apples and junipers are common
SYMPTOMS These diseases produce conspicuous symptoms on both hosts. On pomaceous plants, these include colorful yellow leaf spots with orange borders, fruit and twig galls. In summer, cluster cups containing orange spores erupt from the lower surface of these spots, and from galls. On junipers, symptoms include swollen leaf galls—as big as golf balls—with orange gelatinous tendrils erupting in March, and twig cankers.
DISEASE CYCLE Cedar-apple rust, quince rust, and hawthorn rust are caused by fungi in the genus *Gymnosporangium;* these require two types of plants to complete their 18-month life cycle. Fungal spores produced on one type of plant are carried by wind to infect the other type of plant. Wet spring weather is required for infection of apple foliage and fruit by spores produced on juniper. From midsummer through fall, spores produced on apple are carried by wind to infect juniper.

PREVENTION AND CONTROL
• Choose rust-resistant apples and crabapples.
• Separate junipers and susceptible pomaceous plants—for example, don't put the juniper screen right next to the apple orchard.
• Eliminate rust-susceptible junipers, although this is not practical in areas where junipers are native—including the eastern and western U.S., where junipers are part of the woodland vegetation.   —*EMD*

PEACH LEAF CURL

PLANTS AFFECTED Peach, nectarine, almond; related fungi cause similar diseases in cherry, plum, and oak (oak leaf blister)
REGIONS AFFECTED Peach leaf curl can occur wherever peaches are grown and is more severe where cool, wet weather occurs during early bud development.

Gymnosporangium rust.

Peach leaf curl.

Peaches grown in dry regions of the country are usually not affected.

SYMPTOMS Infected leaves are pale green, reddish, or orange, somewhat thickened, and brittle or leathery. They emerge from the buds curled, puckered, and distorted. Affected leaves eventually develop a whitish bloom of spores on the upper leaf surface.

Phyllosticta leaf spot.

In years of heavy infection, many leaves may drop prematurely. Years of repeated defoliation can severely stress the tree, eventually causing it to die.

DISEASE CYCLE The causal fungus *Taphrina deformans* overwinters on twigs, infecting leaves before they emerge from the buds. Spores produced on leaf surfaces are discharged before the leaves drop, infecting twigs and bud scales. The fungus produces yeast-like spores that are washed to leaf buds by rains.

PREVENTION AND CONTROL

• When planting peaches in a high-risk area, look for resistant cultivars.

• Protect susceptible trees with a fungicide spray such as bordeaux mixture before the leaves emerge. Dormant (after leaf drop) or delayed dormant (before buds swell) applications of copper or lime-sulfur will protect newly emerging leaf buds.   —*MP*

PHYLLOSTICTA LEAF SPOT OF MAPLE

PLANTS AFFECTED Numerous maple species, especially Amur, Japanese, red, and silver maples

REGIONS AFFECTED Throughout the U.S.

SYMPTOMS In early summer, leaves develop roughly circular spots that become tan with purple to red borders. Later in the season, the spots often contain black fruiting bodies of the fungus arrayed in rings inside the lesion. This disease is quite noticeable where maples grow, especially on silver and red maples, but it is mostly of cosmetic concern.

DISEASE CYCLE Infection takes place when airborne fungal spores land on and infect leaves of a susceptible host.

PREVENTION AND CONTROL
• Infection by *Phyllosticta* is localized and leaf damage is usually minimal, so disease probably requires no control.
• Practice good tree care: fertilize, prune, and water during droughts to reduce stress on the trees and increase their resistance to infection.   —*STN*

POWDERY MILDEWS

PLANTS AFFECTED Crabapple, dogwood, London plane tree.
See Diseases of Ornamental Plants, p. 37

SEPTORIA BLIGHT

PLANTS AFFECTED Dogwood.
See Diseases of Ornamental Plants, p. 40

SHOOT/TIP BLIGHTS ON JUNIPERS

PLANTS AFFECTED Many species of junipers.
See Diseases of Ornamental Plants, p. 41

Tar spot.

TAR SPOT OF MAPLE

PLANTS AFFECTED Norway maple, occasionally red, silver, striped, and hedge maples
REGIONS AFFECTED Most common in northeastern U.S.
SYMPTOMS Lesions resembling droplets of tar first appear on leaf surfaces in mid-June as small, pale yellow spots, which enlarge and darken as the season progresses. On red and silver maple, the spots develop a tar-like appearance by late September. On striped and Norway maples, 20 to 50 tiny spots appear on each leaf by early August. On Norway maple, these spots grow and eventually coalesce to form a large black mass. Heavy infections can cause early defoliation.
DISEASE CYCLE The disease is caused by several fungi in the genus *Rhytisma*. Spores overwinter inside spots on infected, fallen leaves. In early spring, the fungal

tissue ripens. The spots split open and minute, needle-like spores are dispersed by wind. If they land on new leaves of a susceptible host they may germinate, penetrate the leaf tissue, and start a new disease cycle.

PREVENTION AND CONTROL

• Rake and destroy infected leaves in the fall to reduce the number of overwintering spots able to cause new infections in the spring.

• Tar spot is rarely serious enough to threaten the health of trees and often no action is required.   —*KLS*

WHITE PINE BLISTER RUST

PLANTS AFFECTED White pines, especially young trees, and plants belonging to the genus *Ribes* (currants and gooseberries)

REGIONS AFFECTED Northeastern U.S.

SYMPTOMS Initial symptoms— small, yellow spots on needles— appear in late summer or autumn. Infection spreads down the needle and into the twig, where slight swelling and yellowing develops during the next growing season. Numerous pale yellow blisters as large as $\frac{1}{10}$-inch across break through the infected bark by mid-May. Blisters disappear after spore discharge, forming again the next year. As the bark dries out

it appears roughened. On *Ribes*, symptoms develop throughout the growing season and are comparatively mild. The lower leaf surface first becomes pale then develops tiny orange, pimple-like fruit bodies.

DISEASE CYCLE Alternate host plants are essential for the perpetuation of the disease. The causal fungus, *Cronartium ribicola*, cannot complete its complicated, five-spore-stage life cycle on white pine or *Ribes* alone. The spores that develop on infected *Ribes* leaves in late summer produce another type of spore that infects pines. The fungus produces two spore stages on pine before returning to *Ribes* to complete its life cycle.

PREVENTION AND CONTROL

• Cut off branches with cankers where they join the next healthy branch. Make cut at least 6 inches beyond the yellowish margin of the canker.

• On trunks, remove all bark 2 inches on each side and 4 inches above and below the canker margin.

• Remove all susceptible *Ribes* from the vicinity of valuable white pines; but note that this will not completely prevent possible infection since spores may be carried by air for several miles.

• If you want to grow *Ribes* as a crop plant, choose resistant cultivars.   —*KLS*

DISEASES OF VEGETABLES

PATRICIA DONALD, WADE H. ELMER, KAREN L. SNOVER

ANTHRACNOSE

PLANTS AFFECTED Vegetables and fruits, especially bean, cucurbits, rose, grape, and brambles
REGIONS AFFECTED Common everywhere but most severe in subtropics
SYMPTOMS Small, water-soaked, slightly sunken circular spots appear on fruit. On tomatoes, this disease is first seen on green fruit, but symptoms are most apparent when the fruit is ripe. As the disease progresses, the spots coalesce, softening and rotting the fruit. Early infections on foliage and young stems usually go undetected and the fungus continues to multiply, spreading to the fruit.
DISEASE CYCLE There are several anthracnose fungi but the most common genus in the garden is *Colletotrichum (Gloeosporium)*. The fungus overwinters on infected plant tissue and spreads via rain splash, wind, infected seed, and human activity.

PREVENTION AND CONTROL
• Use disease-free seed.
• Remove all symptomatic fruit from the garden; warm, humid conditions favor the disease and careful observation of plants when these conditions occur can

Anthracnose on grape leaves.

Bacterial wilt on melons.

limit its spread.
• Limit overhead irrigation.
• Copper and sulfur fungicides and bordeaux mixture are labeled for control of these diseases but their efficacy, restrictions, and phytotoxicity vary with plant species.   —*PD*

BACTERIAL WILT

PLANTS AFFECTED Cucumber and melon (cucumber wilt), corn (Stewart's wilt), bean, and tomato
REGIONS AFFECTED Throughout North America
SYMPTOMS Individual cucumber runners or entire plants wilt and die; plants may recover, but only temporarily. Foliage may yellow.

All growth stages are susceptible. If cut stems are touched together and then pulled apart, stringy bacterial strands form between the cut stem ends. Bacteria may also stream from a cut end when it is placed in a glass of water. Bean seedlings usually die and older plants wilt. In corn, plants wilt and leaves develop long pale streaks. Affected tomatoes usually die without any other symptoms.
DISEASE CYCLE Cucumber beetles are vectors for the bacterium *Erwinia,* which spreads on beetle mouthparts and enters the plant through wounds created when the beetle feeds. The bacteria multiply and enter the xylem vessels, causing disruption of water transport and wilting of the plant. It is unclear how or where the bacteria overwinter. In corn, flea beetles spread the bacterium *Xanthomonas.* In tomato and beans the disease is caused by *Ralstonia (Pseudomonas) solanacearum*; it is soilborne, and moves into plants via water.
PREVENTION AND CONTROL
• Control cucumber beetle vectors (striped and spotted) in cucumber, and flea beetles in corn.
• Remove affected plants.
• Use resistant corn varieties.
                              —*PD*

BOTRYTIS GRAY MOLD

PLANTS AFFECTED Buds and

flowers of vegetables.
See Diseases of Ornamental
Plants, p. 28

CORN SMUT

PLANTS AFFECTED Sweet corn
and some other varieties
REGIONS AFFECTED Wherever
corn is grown
SYMPTOMS Silver swellings or
galls on leaves, individual flowers
in the ear, tassels, or stems,
depending on when the plant was
infected. These growths enlarge
and darken, and eventually break
open to expose masses of black
spores (teliospores).
DISEASE CYCLE The fungus,
Ustilago maydis, overwinters as
spores (teliospores) in crop
debris and in the soil. The spores
can remain viable for several
years. In the spring, the teliospores germinate to produce
basidiospores that move on air
currents or via rainwater and
come in contact with susceptible
corn tissues to repeat the cycle.
The fungus thrives in warm
weather.
PREVENTION AND CONTROL
• Remove smut galls before they
break open and release the spores.
• Seek out resistant varieties.
• Rotate sweet corn yearly. —*PD*

DAMPING-OFF

PLANTS AFFECTED Vegetables.
See Diseases of Ornamental
Plants, p. 30

Corn smut.

DODDER

PLANTS AFFECTED Some vegeta-
bles.
See Diseases of Ornamental
Plants, p. 31

DOWNY MILDEWS

PLANTS AFFECTED Cabbage, cauliflower, cucumber and other
cucurbits, lettuce, onion, and
spinach.
See Diseases of Ornamental
Plants, p. 32

EARLY BLIGHT

PLANTS AFFECTED Celery, car-

Fusarium wilt.

rot, pepper, potato, and tomato. *See* Diseases of Ornamental Plants, p. 33

FUSARIUM WILT

PLANTS AFFECTED Cabbage, celery, muskmelon, pea, potato, spinach, tomato, turnip, and watermelon
REGIONS AFFECTED Wherever susceptible plants are grown, but more common where the soil temperature is between 50°F. and 90°F.
SYMPTOMS When the fungus that causes this disease is present in the soil, the aboveground portion of the plant is stunted, its tissue turns yellow, and the plant wilts around fruiting time.

Vascular stem tissue is discolored near the base of the plant. Young plants usually die.
DISEASE CYCLE The fungus overwinters in plant debris and can survive in soil for a number of years. The fungus moves only short distances via water and soil movement. Long-distance spread of the pathogen happens via infected transplants. Once the fungus reaches susceptible plant root tissue, it spreads through plant cells until it reaches the xylem vessels, and then moves systemically throughout the plant. Xylem vessels become clogged, inhibiting water transport and leading to wilt. When the plant dies, the fungus survives in the plant debris.
PREVENTION AND CONTROL
• Seek out resistant varieties.
• Purchase seeds and plants that are certified as disease-free.
• Once you observe the disease on a particular plant, don't plant members of the same family in that soil or within the root zone of the affected plant.
• Remove symptomatic plants from the garden to avoid buildup of the fungus in the soil.
• Do not overuse nitrogen-based fertilizers.
• Solarize soil.   —*PD*

GUMMY STEM BLIGHT

PLANTS AFFECTED Watermelon, cucumber, cantaloupe, squash, and pumpkin

REGIONS AFFECTED Throughout the U.S.

SYMPTOMS Wilt, leaf spots, and plant death similar to damping-off. Circular, tan to dark brown spots, especially on stems, elongate, crack, and exude a gummy sap. The spots on other plant tissues are dark and enlarge over time. Leaves usually yellow and drop off. Spots on the fruit are yellowish and irregularly circular at first, later turn dark and produce a gummy exudate. Fruit infections often become worse during storage.

DISEASE CYCLE The fungus *Didymella bryoniae (Mycosphaerella melonis)* overwinters in plant debris or in seed. Spores spread to leaves and fruit when plant parts are wet for at least an hour and the temperature is over 70° F.

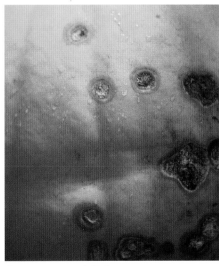

Gummy stem blight.

PREVENTION AND CONTROL
• Do not plant susceptible vine crops in the same part of the garden year after year.
• Gummy stem blight is seed-borne, so a reputable source of seed is a good insurance against the disease.
• Avoid overhead irrigation and watering when the water will remain on the leaves and fruit for hours.   —PD

LATE BLIGHT

PLANTS AFFECTED Tomato and potato

REGIONS AFFECTED Wherever potatoes and tomatoes are grown, except in hot, dry regions

SYMPTOMS Black, water-soaked lesions, sometimes a white fuzzy mass, on leaves and stems of potato and tomato during wet weather. Potato tubers may have brown to purplish lesions with a granular, reddish brown discoloration inside. Tomato fruit may have dark lesions, and the fruit will break down quickly.

DISEASE CYCLE Caused by *Phytophthora infestans*, the disease can be introduced on infected seed potatoes, on plant debris left in the field, and on infected transplants. Spores are dispersed from infected sites by water and with air movement. Wet weather invites severe infections.

DISEASES OF
VEGETABLES

PREVENTION AND CONTROL
• Confirm that composted tomatoes and potatoes have completely decomposed.
• Pull up and destroy any potatoes grown from tubers that overwintered in the garden.
• Plant certified seed potatoes and disease-free tomato plants.
• Plant resistant varieties.
• Examine seed carefully before you plant; discard any with questionable blemishes.
• Mound soil around the base of plants to protect them from spores moving through the soil on flowing water.   —*KLS*

Zucchini yellows virus (mosaic virus).

MOSAIC VIRUSES

PLANTS AFFECTED Cucumber, pea, pepper, tomato, and potato
REGIONS AFFECTED Throughout the U.S.
SYMPTOMS Abnormal growth—dwarfing, stunting—or a reduced yield. Mosaics are mottlings of leaves with light and dark green areas; foliage may also become darker. Leaf blades may be distorted and fernlike. Plants are not usually killed directly by a virus, but their life cycle and productivity are adversely affected.
DISEASE CYCLE The disease spreads via insects, infected seed, and mechanically, via hands or tools. Viruses enter cells through wounds and induce plant cells to go to work making more and more copies of the viruses. Plant symptoms appear when nutrients normally used by the plant are diverted by the virus for its replication.
PREVENTION AND CONTROL
• Remove affected plants.
• Wash tools or hands that come in contact with affected plants with soapy water.
• Reduce virus vectors such as aphids and beetles.
• Plant only transplants, cuttings, or tubers that are certified virus-free.   —*PD*

POWDERY MILDEWS

PLANTS AFFECTED Squash.
See Diseases of Ornamental Plants, p. 37

PYTHIUM ROOT ROT

PLANTS AFFECTED Vegetables and herbs.
See Diseases of Ornamental Plants, p. 38

ROOT-KNOT NEMATODES

PLANTS AFFECTED Carrot, parsnip, potato, tomato, pepper, melon
REGIONS AFFECTED Throughout the U.S.

Root-knot nematode galls.

SYMPTOMS Growth is poor; stunting, yellowish foliage and wilting when moisture is adequate, fruit ripens unevenly, plant sometimes dies. In roots or underground plant parts, galls—plant growths formed in response to nematodes—may be present by the time aboveground symptoms are seen.
DISEASE CYCLE There are several species of root-knot nematodes (in the genus *Meloidogyne*) that attack garden vegetables. The species common in the South produces bigger galls and can be more destructive; but northern species can also cause plant damage. Nematodes enter roots from infested soil and establish a feeding site within root tissue. Nematodes reproduce and spread within the roots as long as adequate plant material is available.
PREVENTION AND CONTROL
• Check transplants for root galls.
• Remove affected plants; do not compost.
• Rotate plants.
• Plant tomatoes resistant to root-knot nematode; these will have an "N" on the seed packet.
• Relocate your vegetable garden if the site is infested with root-knot nematodes.
• Plant early and short-season crops to reduce the buildup of root-knot nematodes.   *—PD*

SEPTORIA BLIGHT

PLANTS AFFECTED Celery, eggplant, and tomato.
See Diseases of Ornamental Plants, p. 40

SOUTHERN BLIGHT

PLANTS AFFECTED A large number of vegetables.
See Diseases of Ornamental Plants, p. 41

DISEASES OF VEGETABLES

Verticillium wilt.

VERTICILLIUM WILT

PLANTS AFFECTED A wide variety of plants including tomato, beet, eggplant, pepper, potato, sunflower, strawberry, potato, and several herbs
REGIONS AFFECTED Wherever host plants are grown
SYMPTOMS Older leaves wilt, turn yellow, and die. Scraping the stem near the ground reveals a dark discoloration. Symptoms can resemble *Fusarium* wilt.
DISEASE CYCLE The fungus is soilborne, and overwinters in soils as resting structures called microsclerotia, which survive as minor parasites on the roots of plants that are not susceptible. Root infection occurs when young roots grow near the fungus. The fungus invades the water-conducting tissues and ascends into the stem, causing chlorosis, wilt, and death.
PREVENTION AND CONTROL
• Choose resistant varieties if available.
• Mulch and fertilize to suppress the disease.
• Rotate with non-susceptible crops, such as corn for at least two years.
• Solarize soil.   —*WHE*

WHITE MOLD

PLANTS AFFECTED Vegetables. *See* Diseases of Ornamental Plants, p. 43

WHITE SMUT

PLANTS AFFECTED Spinach. *See* Diseases of Ornamental Plants, p. 44

DISEASES OF TURFGRASS

KAREN L. SNOVER

BROWN PATCH

PLANTS AFFECTED Bentgrass, ryegrass, annual bluegrass, and tall fescues; less often Kentucky bluegrass and fine fescues
REGIONS AFFECTED Throughout North America
SYMPTOMS Symptoms depend largely on type of grass, mowing practices, and moisture levels. When mowed closely and kept wet, cool-season grasses may produce blighted patches up to 20 inches across that may have a purplish gray border—a "smoke-ring." Cool-season grasses cut higher can produce small, light brown patches up to 20 inches in diameter that may exhibit the smoke-ring. A patch known as a "frog-eye" may also appear: apparently healthy green grass is surrounded by a sunken ring of flat, dead grass. Individual leaf lesions may be small, round to irregularly shaped, and tan with a distinctive dark brown margin.
DISEASE CYCLE The fungus

Rhizoctonia solani infects plants from June through early July. *R. zeae* takes *R. solani*'s place as summer arrives. Optimum temperature for fungal germination is 70°F.–90°F.
PREVENTION AND CONTROL
• Reduce thatch (accumulation of dying grass and other organic matter buildup).
• Remove dew from the leaf blades.
• Increase mowing height.

Brown patch.

Fairy ring.

Symptoms are not as severe or noticeable on higher cut grass, and the grass tends to be less stressed and can therefore help itself in competing with the pathogen.
• Provide good drainage conditions.
• Monitor fertilizer applications to ensure adequate but not excessive nitrogen levels, which can increase disease occurrence and severity.
• Seek out resistant cultivars.

FAIRY RING

PLANTS AFFECTED Most grass species
REGIONS AFFECTED Throughout North America
SYMPTOMS Circles or arcs of lush grass or mushrooms appear in lawn. Most rings are between 20 inches and 16 feet, but can expand to 65 feet.
DISEASE CYCLE Lush growth is

caused by nutrients, especially nitrogen, released by fungi in the soil. Small rings appear initially; these become larger each year as the fungus grows in a radial pattern. Rings can increase in size as much as 20 inches annually and can become quite large after many years.
PREVENTION AND CONTROL
• Some mushrooms are very poisonous when eaten; destroy any that might be attractive to small children or pets.
• If ring consists only of mushrooms or puffballs, simply rake off and dispose of these fungal fruiting structures to improve the appearance of the lawn.
• Disguise the symptoms by providing adequate water deep into the root zone in the area of the ring and by moderate fertilization; excessive fertilization may contribute to other disease problems.
• Mow frequently to make the difference in height between grass of the fairy ring and adjacent grass less conspicuous.

RED THREAD

PLANTS AFFECTED Bluegrasses, fescues, ryegrasses, and bentgrasses; fine-leaved fescues and some ryegrasses are particularly susceptible
REGIONS AFFECTED Humid and cool-temperate regions
SYMPTOMS Water-soaked patches of grass die and fade to a

Red thread on bluegrass.

Stem rust.

bleach-tan color when dry. Irregularly shaped or circular patches to 14 inches in diameter may appear scorched. Patches may be widely scattered or coalesce into larger spots. In humid weather, the fungus produces pink to red hyphae protruding upward from the tips of brown grass blades, hence the name "red-thread disease."

DISEASE CYCLE Red thread occurs in humid periods in spring and fall when temperatures are between 60°F. and 75°F. Disease is especially severe on slow-growing, nitrogen-deficient turf. The fungus *Laetisaria fuciformis* spreads when infected tissue and "red threads" move to healthy areas on mowing equipment, through foot traffic, and other activities. Spores are a secondary means of dispersal.

PREVENTION AND CONTROL
• Maintain adequate soil fertility.
• Avoid overwatering, and don't

water in late afternoon or evening.
• Provide good soil drainage.
• Space trees and shrubs so that large areas of grass are not shaded for long periods; selective pruning of established trees and shrubs can help.
• Reduce thatch.
• Plant resistant varieties.
• Some organic fertilizers will reduce disease severity.

RUST

PLANTS AFFECTED All turfgrass species
REGIONS AFFECTED Anywhere cool- and warm-season grasses are grown
SYMPTOMS Yellow lesions initially, enlarging over time. Mature spores break through the lesions and are blown or splashed to new sites. Spore pustules (blister-like spots created as spores form underneath and push out-

ward) are usually orange, but may appear yellow, red, or brown. In severe cases, stands of grass may be very thin and discolored.

DISEASE CYCLE Rust diseases have a very complicated five spore-stage life cycle often involving two alternating hosts. The spore stage, with characteristic orange pustules, is most damaging; the spores reproduce and cause new infections as often as every two weeks. On the alternate host (often barberry), the fungus produces two spore stages before returning to turfgrass to complete its life cycle.

PREVENTION AND CONTROL
• Water early in the day to encourage quick drying; irrigate deeply and infrequently.
• Avoid drought and poor drainage.
• Mow often and increase mowing height.
• Rake up clippings when the disease is present and discard or destroy them.
• Prune surrounding trees to provide more light and better air circulation.
• Use resistant varieties when available.

SUMMER PATCH

PLANTS AFFECTED Kentucky bluegrass, annual bluegrass, fescue, and bentgrass
REGIONS AFFECTED Anywhere cool- and warm-season grasses are grown

SYMPTOMS Scattered, light green patches develop during summer. Patches turn tan to reddish brown, growing to 30 inches in diameter. A frog-eye— apparently healthy green grass surrounded by a ring of dead grass—may appear. Blighted areas often occur near sidewalks, driveways, buildings, sites in direct sun, and south-facing slopes. The disease is likely to recur each year and increase in intensity.

DISEASE CYCLE The fungus *Magnaporthe poae* overwinters in plant tissue or debris. Infection takes place in late spring. Symptoms appear when temperatures rise during wet weather. The fungus may spread from root to root, or on infected plant material and mechanical equipment.

PREVENTION AND CONTROL
• Correct excess soil acidity by spreading lime annually to maintain a pH level above 6.2.
• Fertilize only in autumn and late spring.
• Water disease-prone areas to a depth of 6–8 inches every seven to ten days during the dry periods of summer.
• Mow frequently to a height of 2–4 inches, removing less than a third of the leaf blade each time.
• Reduce thatch.
• Plant resistant cultivars.

ENCYCLOPEDIA OF PLANT DISORDERS

The following encyclopedia addresses the major disorders, or non-infectious diseases, that may crop up in your garden. Disorders are brought on by environmental factors, rather than specific pathogens. They develop in direct response to environmental conditions or stresses affecting the quality of light or air, as well as the availability of nutrients or water.

PLANT DISORDERS

MARGERY DAUGHTREY, PATRICIA DONALD

AIR POLLUTION

If you live in an area with poor air quality, your plants may be stressed by air pollution. One of the most common forms is ozone injury, which occurs most dramatically during hot summer months. Generally speaking, levels of ozone, a product of vehicle exhaust, are much higher in densely populated areas. Plants especially susceptible to ozone are Eastern white pine, morning glories, beans, grapes, and petunias. Other forms of pollution are more likely to be localized. Sulfur dioxide (SO_2) injury, for example, can form if a sulfur-containing fuel source (such as coal) is

Ozone injury.

burned nearby. Clover, violet, apple, white pine, lettuce, and sunflower are notably sensitive to sulfur dioxide.

SYMPTOMS Some symptoms are subtle—stunting and enhanced susceptibility to disease. Ozone-susceptible plants often exhibit a purplish flecking or discoloration on their leaves; they may also exhibit bleaching of the upper leaf surface. The injury is most pronounced on newly matured leaves: young and old leaves may escape injury because they do not have functional stomata. SO_2 injury typically appears as dry, white or tan patches between leaf veins, particularly on middle-aged leaves.

PREVENTION AND CONTROL There is no way to manage the symptoms of air pollution on plants. Learn to recognize symptoms, so that you don't mistakenly apply a pesticide.   *—MD*

CHLORINE INJURY

Chlorine used to sanitize both indoor and outdoor pools can injure nearby plants. Chlorine fumes can concentrate in indoor pool areas, damaging foliage; plants that are splashed with chlorinated water outdoors can suffer stress or be killed. Chlorine injury can also result when de-icing salts are used around plants.

SYMPTOMS Yellowing and leaf drop.

PREVENTION AND CONTROL
• Try different kinds of interiorscape plants to find those that can tolerate chlorine fumes.
• Install vents for air exchange.
• Outdoors, do not locate sensitive plants in areas where pool drainage or de-icing salt spray could be a problem.   *—MD*

DROUGHT STRESS

Common garden plants grown in light, sandy soils that retain little moisture will often show signs of drought stress when rainfall or irrigation has been insufficient.

SYMPTOMS Stunting, leaf-edge scorch, wilting, predisposition to winter injury or disease, and death.

PREVENTION AND CONTROL
• Grow plants suited to the soil moisture conditions in your garden. Such plants will require supplemental irrigation in the first, and sometimes the second, growing season, but in the long run they will need watering only during a protracted drought.
• Learn the moisture needs of the different plants in your garden, and group plants according to water needs.
• Incorporate organic matter into the soil and mulch to increase moisture retention around plants.
• Use a rain gauge to increase your awareness of natural rainfall. When rainfall is not adequate, supplemental irrigation will maintain plant vigor. One

Leaves damaged by drought.

common rule of thumb is to irrigate when there has been less than 1 inch of rain during a 7-day period; this will vary with soil type, however.

• Test sprinklers or trickle-irrigation systems to learn how long it takes them to provide the equivalent of 1 inch of rainfall. Use a glass jar with a ruler in it to time the delivery of a given depth of water. Dig into the soil after a timed irrigation period to see how far down the water has penetrated.

• Water only to the depth needed by the plants (e.g., to 6 inches for turf; deeper for woody ornamentals). Thorough watering is more beneficial than frequent light watering.

• To avoid fostering foliar diseases, water early in the day to allow foliage to dry before nightfall.   —*MD*

EDEMA

Edema is the term used for tiny blisters that appear on leaves, most often on the leaf undersides. It is associated with overwatering and factors related to the quality of light. Individual cells swell and often burst, leaving a small corky spot. Edema may occur on houseplants.

SYMPTOMS Outdoors it is most often observed on ivy geraniums, some cultivars of which will develop such severe edema that even the upper leaf surface becomes unattractive. Although edema is a physiological disorder, the symptoms are very similar to those of spider-mite feeding injury—so look for mites with a hand lens before you assume that your plant has edema.

PREVENTION AND CONTROL
• Make sure that hanging baskets of ivy geraniums are allowed to drain after watering, so that excess water isn't retained in the saucer. Keep them well fertilized.
• Ask your garden center or florist to recommend ivy geranium cultivars that are less prone to edema. —*MD*

FLOODING INJURY

If the soil around a plant is flooded, its root system will be deprived of oxygen. If this condition endures, the plant will die. Flooding creates very favorable conditions for the water mold fungi *Pythium* and *Phytophthora*,

so if flooding persists or occurs frequently, plants may be killed indirectly by root-rotting fungi.
SYMPTOMS Wilting, stunting, and/or death of plants.
PREVENTION AND CONTROL Locate moisture-intolerant plants in well-drained parts of the garden, and plant only species adapted to a swampier existence in areas where periodic flooding is anticipated. Do not overwater. —*MD*

FREEZING/CHILLING INJURY

Freezing or chilling injury can manifest itself in many different ways, depending on the hardiness of the plant and the rapidity and extent of the cold stress.
SYMPTOMS Chilled herbaceous plants may have dark spots or bleached areas on leaves or flowers; they may develop grayish

Leaf underside affected by edema.

Winter damage on *Mahonia*.

PLANT DISORDERS

Herbicide damage on soybean leaf.

off-color foliage, or wilt and collapse completely and dramatically. Woody plants may show leaf spotting, small holes in the leaves, or shoot blight from a late frost. In cold winters without protective snow-cover, some tender species may perish where they have thrived for years. Woody plants with thin bark such as azaleas, fruit trees, and ornamental cherries are the most prone to trunk- or stem-splitting from sharp temperature drops. This injury usually appears as a vertical fissure in the bark on the southwest side of the tree.

PREVENTION AND CONTROL
• Plant species that are hardy for your area; plant these in the appropriate soil type with the right amount of shade.
• Plants of borderline hardiness should be located in sheltered sites, out of the wind.
• Burlap or other fabrics may be used to screen sensitive ever-greens (such as boxwoods) from winter desiccation.
• Mulch around the base of trees, but do not bring the mulch all the way to the trunk.
• Irrigate during dry spells in the fall; drought stress will increase winter injury.
• Fertilize trees in early spring. In fall, fertilize only after trees have gone into dormancy, but while the soil is still over 40°F.
• Remember that plants grown in containers may need extra protection to survive winter cold.

—MD

HERBICIDE INJURY

Herbicide damage is most commonly caused by lawn fertilizers that contain growth-regulating (phenoxy) herbicides or when treated lawn clippings are applied as mulch in the garden.

SYMPTOMS Exposure to phenoxy-type herbicides commonly used to control lawn weeds (2-4, D) causes abnormal leaf growth—curling of the leaf tips and veins growing closely together in a parallel fashion in especially sensitive plants, such as tomatoes and grapes. These symptoms can be confused with viral infections, but viruses may affect only a few plants or only members of a particular family, whereas herbicide damage is usually more widespread. Dicamba, another commonly used lawn herbicide, causes abnormal growth and can cause fiddle-head of potato.

PREVENTION AND CONTROL
• Do not apply lawn herbicides or fertilizers containing herbicides to gardens.
• Do not use herbicide-treated grass clippings as mulch in the garden. Do not put herbicide-treated grass clippings in the compost pile, as some herbicides do not break down in composting.   —*PD*

IRON DEFICIENCY

Iron deficiency is a problem in regions where soils are alkaline (having a pH above 7.0). Although some kinds of plants prefer this soil chemistry, others will develop trace element deficiencies when the pH is too high. Iron deficiency is one of the most dramatic of these.

SYMPTOMS The first sign is yellowing between the veins on the new leaves. The veins remain green as the leaves yellow. Scarlet, pin, and red oaks may all show iron chlorosis when the pH is above 6.5. Ericaceous plants (such as azalea, rhododendron, mountain laurel, and blueberry) need pH 4.5–5.5 for best growth.

PREVENTION AND CONTROL
• Choose plants that are suited to your soil pH (take a clue from the native vegetation in the area).
• Trying to grow acid-loving plants in an alkaline soil could prove difficult, especially with those that develop deep root sys-

Rhododendron with iron deficiency.

tems. It may be possible to grow plants with a compact, fibrous root system if you incorporate peat moss or acid muck from swamps in the soil, or treat with elemental sulfur; test periodically to maintain proper soil pH.
• Choose a fertilizer specifically formulated for acid-loving plants (e.g. with ammonium nitrate as the nitrogen source).
• Supply iron in an iron chelate spray or drench.
• Mulch with pine needles or composted oak leaves, which help acidify the soil.
• Do not amend the soil with alkaline materials such as wood ashes, bone meal, or lime.

—*MD*

PLANT DISORDERS

IRON/MANGANESE TOXICITY

Excess of some trace elements can be just as harmful as deficiency. These levels are primarily regulated by the soil pH: if the pH is below 6.0, iron and manganese are extremely available to plants, and some species will take up toxic overdoses.

SYMPTOMS On French marigolds and some varieties of geraniums, tiny brown to black or purple flecks develop in the lower to middle leaves, and the leaves may turn yellow or brown along the margins.

PREVENTION AND CONTROL
• Apply lime to raise the soil pH to 6.0; you can use dolomitic or calcitic (ground) limestone.
• Use fertilizers with calcium nitrate as the nitrogen source.
—*MD*

NITROGEN DEFICIENCY

Nitrogen is one of the major elements required for plant growth. It may be deficient in some soils because it is easily leached away through rainfall or irrigation.

SYMPTOMS Lower leaves will turn yellow and plants will be stunted in comparison to well-fertilized plants of the same type.

PREVENTION AND CONTROL
Most organic and inorganic fertilizers include a nitrogen component (the N in the N-P-K formulation listed on the product label).

You should supply sufficient nitrogen for productivity and growth, but too much can reduce flowering or fruit harvest and can make plants more susceptible to diseases or insect pests. Before undertaking extensive vegetable or flower gardening, get a complete analysis of the pH, salts, and nutrients in your soil so that you can fertilize appropriately. Apply only the recommended amount of fertilizer.
—*MD*

SALT INJURY

The sodium chloride and calcium chloride used to melt ice on roads, driveways, and walkways can injure trees. Salt water can contaminate wells at the seaside, and if this well water is used for irrigation, it can harm plants. Even salts in fertilizers are harmful to plants if supplied in excess: high levels of soluble salts will damage root tips, especially when the soil is dry.

SYMPTOMS Conifers may show brown tip dieback and decline; deciduous trees may show stunted growth, branch dieback, and scorching along leaf margins.

PREVENTION AND CONTROL
• Use plant-friendly alternatives (such as sand or cinders) to make icy walkways near valuable plants passable.
• Be sure drainage is sufficient in areas where valuable ornamentals are located—salts are

Salt damage.

Sooty mold.

water-soluble and will readily leach with rain or watering.
• Relocate walkways that need to be salted farther from valuable specimen plants. Plant salt-tolerant trees and shrubs (*Rosa rugosa*, *Pinus mugo*, *Picea pungens*, and *Quercus alba*, for example) in locations where salt spray is unavoidable. Plant salt-sensitive plants such as white pine (*Pinus strobus*) and red and sugar maples (*Acer rubrum* and *A. saccharum*) 30 yards from a roadway where de-icing salt is used.
• Protect heavily fertilized plants from drought stress.
• Test irrigation water to be sure that the soluble-salts level is below 525 ppm.   —*MD*

SOOTY MOLD

Sooty mold is caused by aphids and other sucking insects: they consume excessive amounts of plant sap, which is excreted as honeydew. The sweet, sticky honeydew becomes food for fungi, which grow very visibly upon leaf, stem, and flower surfaces, but cause no real harm to the plant.
SYMPTOMS Sooty mold is not a disease, but it is often mistaken for one. The black deposit on leaf surfaces is not physically attached to the leaf and is easily wiped off.
PREVENTION AND CONTROL
• Sooty mold can be rubbed off leaves with your fingers, and sometimes can be dislodged with a jet of water from the watering hose.
• Look on the plant itself and on overhanging plants or trees for the real culprit. You will probably find mealybugs, scale insects, aphids, or other sucking insects. Populations of these can often be controlled with insecticidal soap or horticultural-oil sprays at the appropriate time of the year: seek assistance from your local Co-operative Extension office for identification of the pest and the correct timing for its control.   —*MD*

PLANT DISORDERS

NINE KEYS TO DISEASE PREVENTION

JIM CHATFIELD

PREVENTION IS THE ESSENCE of plant-disease control. This is true whether a disease is infectious (involving host-parasite relationships between plants and pathogens such as certain fungi, bacteria, or viruses) or non-infectious (involving disorders such as nutrient deficiencies or winter damage). As with human ailments, plant diseases are best stopped before they start. Even if you resort to fungicides to control disease, you are probably practicing a form of prevention because most must be applied before infectious agents arrive. Following are nine key ways to prevent diseases before they start.

1. UNDERSTAND THE DISEASE TRIANGLE.

The first step in prevention is to have a good understanding of infectious disease. The simple but extremely useful concept of the disease triangle is fundamental to that understanding. Diseases can occur only when the following three components are present at the same time:
- A susceptible *host plant*
- A *pathogen* capable of causing disease
- An *environment* conducive to disease

The disease triangle is also a creative way to remind yourself of the different ways to prevent disease: break the links in the triangle at any point and disease will not occur. For example, if you plant the susceptible crabapple *Malus* 'Radiant' in an area where the apple scab fungus *Venturia inaequalis* is abundant, and spring is very moist, all three components of the disease triangle are in place, and the tree will likely develop significant scab disease. But if you plant a disease-resistant cultivar such as *Malus*

To minimize disease problems, pick the right plants for the site. Unlike other hollies, winterberry holly thrives in swampy conditions.

'Prairiefire', you don't provide a susceptible host—and can avoid infection. Another way to break a link in the disease triangle is to exclude pathogens. Removing blighted potato tubers from the garden at the end of the season limits the amount of fungal inoculum (pathogen tissue responsible for causing infection) available for the next season. Cleaning up black-spotted rose leaves in the fall reduces the amount of black spot fungal inoculum. Or you can adopt cultural practices that make the environment less conducive to infection. If you avoid overhead watering, for example, you discourage infection by foliar pathogens that thrive on damp leaves.

2. CHOOSE THE RIGHT PLANTS.

One of the most important things you can do to prevent disease is to select the right plant for the site—which is much easier than trying to manage a problem-plagued plant in an unsuitable site later. Proper plant selection will help prevent both non-infectious and many infectious diseases that are more likely to occur and be more severe if plants are stressed. With prevention timing is everything, so start thinking about it even before you plant.

Read the site. Learn as much as you can about the different parts of your garden before planting. What is currently growing there? What plants are thriving on nearby, similar sites? Learn what parts of your garden drain poorly. Observe the site at different times to understand the sun and wind exposures. You can learn a great deal about the general soil pH range by noting how acid-loving plants such as pachysandra, rhododendrons, and red maple fare in your garden and nearby areas.

Test the site. Soil pH is a determining factor when deciding what to plant. For failing to foot the cost of a $10 or $15 soil test, many have paid later. Some acid-loving plants will grow reasonably well for years as they reap the benefits of the soil in their root ball, but then begin to decline as they encounter more and more of the native alkaline soil. This is a very avoidable scenario. Don't guess—soil test!

Know your plants. Don't make assumptions about plant tolerances in general; find out how the varieties that you want to plant tolerate sun, wind, and various soil conditions. Many people say, for example, that hollies will not tolerate wet, poorly drained sites. This is indeed true of American holly (*Ilex opaca*) or the Meserve blue and China series hybrids (*Ilex × meserveae*), which are quite susceptible to black root rot disease in wet sites. It is not true of the deciduous winterberry holly (*Ilex verticillata*), which thrives in swampy sites.

Find out about common problems. Get a handle on the diseases of the

Before planting, test the soil. The most reliable way to do this is by taking a soil sample from your garden and sending it to a soil test lab for analysis.

plants you want to grow. Every plant has a profile of characteristic disease problems that develop in a particular area. Many plants are also sensitive to environmental conditions. White pine is highly sensitive to roadside salt spray, and sugar maples decline when highway salt concentrates in surrounding soils. Broad-leaved evergreens such as rhododendrons and mahonias suffer desiccation and leaf scorch when exposed to drying winter winds.

Learn how plants interact. Plants interact with each other in ways that are important to consider when planning your garden. A spectacular example of this is allelopathy, a kind of chemical warfare that can exist between plants, and can cause non-infectious diseases. Black walnuts produce a chemical called juglone, especially in their roots, that is toxic to many other plants. Tomatoes growing within the root zone of black walnuts, which can extend well beyond the drip line of the tree, are especially susceptible; they will wilt and die when exposed to juglone.

A more mundane type of plant interaction is competition for water, nutrients, and sunlight. All too often, landscape trees are planted too closely together. Over the years, this results in excessive shading, and root competition for water and minerals, leading to stressed plants and greater susceptibility to opportunistic fungal pathogens (which cause serious harm only on plants that are already stressed). *Cytospora* canker of spruce, for example, is more common and causes larger cankers when spruces are suffering from drought. Proper plant spacing will limit such problems and help prevent diseases in the long term.

3. USE DISEASE-RESISTANT PLANTS.

Selecting plants with genetic disease resistance is the best way to prevent disease. If your crabapples get scab disease and lose much of their foliage in moist springs, start planting resistant cultivars such as 'Bob White' or 'Red Jewel', so you don't have to spend your days spraying fungicides.

No plant will be completely disease-free—that's a myth. But some plants have fewer major disease problems. Make use of all available information on the disease resistance of those plants that you decide to add to your garden. Check out the references at the end of this book on page 104. Ask your fellow plant-lovers which varieties work for them and if plant societies they may belong to have compiled specialized lists. Read the commentary in garden catalogs and on seed packets. Get information from your local garden center, arboreta, and botanical gardens, or the Extension Service in your state. Consult specialized publications for extensive lists of resistant cultivars.

At planting time, bear in mind the size of the fully grown plant. Trees suffer from excessive shading and competition for water and minerals, leading to stressed plants that are susceptible to disease.

A word of warning: lists of disease-resistant cultivars can be useful, but take them with a grain of salt. Do not assume that any list is definitive. You may find maples listed as susceptible to *Verticillium* wilt, but Japanese maple (*Acer palmatum*) is considerably more susceptible than many other maples. Lists are sometimes only locally accurate. Roses that are highly susceptible to black spot in one part of the country may be resistant in another area because the fungal pathogen may have mutated there. These mutants may in turn infect rose cultivars that were previously resistant. And they may be present in one part of the country only—at least for a while.

Lists of disease-resistant cultivars may also ignore a plant's other good—or bad—qualities. Two lists developed by Ohio botanists rated crabapples for susceptibility to scab, as well as for overall aesthetics—flower, foliage, fruit, form, and other features. Eight of the ten most aesthetically pleasing crabapples had some scab, but not enough to affect their overall appeal; seven of the ten scab-free crabapples were in the bottom half of the overall ratings. So, take everything into account, not just disease resistance, when selecting plants.

4. KEEP UP WITH GARDEN CLEAN-UP.

Eliminating the pathogen that can cause disease is a time-honored approach to disease prevention. Late blight of potato is the fungal disease that contributed greatly to the Irish potato famine of the 1840s–50s, rotting entire crops in the field or in storage. Potato growers quickly learned the importance of cleaning up diseased potatoes at the end of the season to limit the amount of fungus in the soil the following season. Sanitation for disease control is just as important today. The fungus that causes rose black spot overwinters on black-spotted leaves from the previous season's infestations and on infected rose canes. Remove diseased leaves and canes from the garden to keep black spot from getting a start on the new season. If disease does develop, remove the black-spotted leaves during the season to slow the repeating cycle of this disease throughout the spring and summer.

An extreme form of sanitation is called roguing: removing infested plants as soon as they are noted. This is typically done with serious diseases such as orange rust of brambles. Any plants exhibiting this rust disease, including wild brambles, should immediately be removed and destroyed before the fungus spreads to healthy plants.

You should also practice a form of roguing before purchasing plants. If you are buying containerized plants or bedding plants, gently knock the plant from its container and check the root system. Look for healthy light-colored roots. Blackish and slimy roots are a sign of poor root health and

Always remove diseased plant material from the garden. Many pathogens can overwinter on plant debris, reinfecting new growth in the following year.

root rot disease. Check plants such as roses, stone fruits, and euonymus for bacterial crown gall, tumor-like growths on roots and crowns. Under certain circumstances, harvesting seed from your garden for future years can be risky, because you may also be saving pathogens that hitch a ride on those seeds, which will cause you problems later.

Rotating crops is another way to prevent disease. Many soilborne pathogens remain in the ground for a considerable time, often for many years. So, in order to save susceptible plants from a pathogen, you want to separate the two. For example, if you have plants that have been diagnosed with *Verticillium* wilt, assume that the soil is infested with *Verticillium* fungus. When replanting, site the plants in a different location—where the soil may not be infested with the pathogen.

Don't forget to use common sense with your sanitation practices. When you are pruning, make cuts on healthy tissue first, and prune out diseased tissue last. When dealing with highly infectious diseases such as fire blight, sanitize tools with alcohol between pruning cuts. Clean and remove soil from tools periodically. When you have problems with soilborne diseases such as damping-off in your seedling trays, remove the potting soil from the seeding area and sanitize the surface with a bleach solution.

5. CREATE WELL-BALANCED SOIL.

What gardeners typically see when a good plant goes bad are its scorched and discolored leaves, and twigs and branches that decline and die. More often than not these aboveground symptoms are caused by problems with the root system.

What makes for a happy root system? For many plants, the key is a moist but well-drained soil rich in organic matter. In such soils—the kind you can ball up in your hand and crumble but which does not form a ball of clay—there is both adequate air and adequate moisture for the roots to properly respire. In good soils, inorganic clay, silt, and sand particles form aggregates with organic matter, allowing optimal nutrient exchange between soil particles, the soil solution (water with dissolved minerals and associated microorganisms), and plant roots.

Soils with good texture and good organic matter content also tend to have a healthy balance of soil organisms, from earthworms to bacterial and fungal microorganisms that cycle nutrients. These will coexist with other soil microorganisms that can cause plant problems, such as disease-causing root-rotting fungi. All these organisms exist in the soil in a precarious balance, which can go haywire when major environmental stresses change the equation. The best balance will be achieved by developing

Add at least an inch of compost over all growing areas in spring, and work the compost into the top several inches of soil. Soils with good overall texture and drainage characteristics and good organic matter content tend to have a healthy balance of soil organisms, from earthworms to bacterial and fungal microorganisms, that cycle nutrients.

soils that have good overall texture and drainage characteristics and good organic matter content, which will optimize microbial activity.

Adding compost to your soil will help you achieve these goals. Add at least an inch of compost over all growing areas before you plant in the spring, and work the compost into the top several inches of soil. Side-dress heavy-feeding crops such as squash, corn, tomatoes, and broccoli with an additional half-inch layer of compost each month during the growing season.

People in climates with prolonged sunny stretches can solarize soils, i.e. use the heat of the sun to eliminate pathogens. Cultivate the soil to a depth of at least 4 inches. Water the soil well, then cover with clear plastic at least 1.5 mm (0.0015 inch) thick and bury and anchor the edges in a trench around the bed. At least six weeks of abundant sunshine are needed for effective solarization, which kills not only pathogens, but also beneficial organisms. That's not the only drawback. The technique will eliminate pathogens in only the top few inches of soil, probably not to the full depth of plant roots. And solarized soil is easily recontaminated. How-

Avoid wetting plant leaves during irrigation to discourage foliar pathogens that thrive on damp leaves—for example, by using a soaker hose.

ever, beneficial organisms such as *Trichoderma* species tend to prefer solarized soil for recolonizing, and biocontrol agents can be mixed with seeds or added to the soil when transplanting to maximize benefits.

6. KEEP YOUR PLANTS HEALTHY.

With proper plant care, you can limit the amount of stress your plants suffer and the likelihood that they will develop certain infectious and non-infectious diseases.

Proper planting should be one of the first considerations. Be sure to plant trees and shrubs at the same grade that they were grown in the nursery or garden center. If installed too high, their root systems may dry out, but planting too low is even worse: it is the primary cause of transplant shock of many trees and shrubs in the first few years after planting. The deeper you go in the soil, the lower the concentration of oxygen, and the greater the chance of root stress. Plants already stressed by the loss of roots during the transplanting process, or by root scoring if they were grown in containers, may not be able to bear the additional stress of a too-deep planting.

Once plants are installed, proper watering is crucial. Though many people assume that watering is easy, there are no simple rules for irrigation, so this is one of the most difficult and essential green-thumb skills to develop. Plants have individual needs that depend on the species, the size of the plant, and its stage of development. Soil type and weather conditions also come into play. Too little water can stress plants, making them more susceptible to disease organisms such as canker fungi. Excessive watering results in poor overall root function and greater susceptibility to root rot diseases. And if you water in a way that keeps moisture on a plant's leaves for long periods, you may be encouraging infection by foliar pathogens. So if you use a sprinkler or other overhead irrigation system, water early in the day when moisture is more likely to evaporate from leaf surfaces. Do not assume that plants need water. Check the soil to a depth of several inches to determine if it is still wet. For most plants, it is best to wait until the soil dries and then water deeply. Many plants, including your lawn, need about one inch of moisture per week during the growing season. Use common sense when deciding which plants might need water. For example, check seedbeds more often than sites with established plants.

Mulching is a crucial disease prevention practice. Organic mulches provide many benefits: they help cool soils and conserve and moderate moisture over long periods, which can help plants resist stress due to lack of water. Moisture and temperature modification are crucial for the roots of many plants, especially if they are a bit out of their optimal soil temperature range, such as mountain ashes, flowering dogwoods, and exotic birches in hot, open sites. Over time, organic mulches such as composted bark mulches also provide important organic matter for the soil and can help control diseases by encouraging microorganisms that may act as biological controls of plant pathogens. Mulches can also help prevent noninfectious diseases: a good 2- to 3-inch deep ring of mulch around the base of plants (but pulled away from direct contact with the trunk) will suppress weeds and keep the lawn mower at a safe distance from vulnerable plant tissue.

Pruning is another important disease preventive. When you cut away the knotted, black, gall-like growths from the stems of stone-fruit trees and ornamental plants infected with plum black knot, you are removing pathogens and the inoculum they provide for subsequent infections. Prune when you first notice the disease; if you wait too long, pruning will not be effective. Through proper pruning you can also keep a tree's inner foliage from becoming too dense, assuring better air movement and sun penetration of the canopy. Most fungi thrive under moist conditions, and fungal spores are more likely to germinate and infect leaf tissue when leaves remain wet.

Pruning is an important disease preventive. Remove diseased stems as soon as you notice them. With highly infectious diseases, sanitize tools with alcohol between cuts.

Fertilizing plants will both prevent non-infectious diseases (disorders), such as nutrient deficiencies, and help plants tolerate the damage resulting from infectious diseases. Make sure to choose the proper fertilizer for your particular plant to promote sustainable growth and plant survival. Fertilizers are not magic—and they are not "plant food." They cannot replace the food that plants produce in their leaves, but they can provide much-needed minerals such as nitrogen, phosphorus, and potassium (NPK) and micronutrients like copper, iron, and manganese.

7. DO NO HARM.

You can overdo many good horticultural practices, and in some cases invite the very same diseases you are working to avert.

Take the case of mulching. The merits of this practice are undeniable, so how can such a good thing go wrong? The answer lies in the increasingly popular habit of amassing huge mounds of mulch—sometimes to depths of 6 inches, a foot, even several feet—around the bases of trees

Mulching helps regulate the moisture and temperature of the soil and prevents weed growth. Maintain a 2- to 3-inch layer of mulch in your garden beds, making sure to keep mulch well away from the bases of trees and shrubs.

and shrubs. This keeps too much moisture against trunks, encouraging fungal infections. It also provides perfect cover for rabbits, mice, and other rodents in the winter, little havens from which they can munch on thin-barked plants at their leisure. Excessive mulch can reduce oxygen levels in the soil, leading to poor root metabolism and increased root rot disease. Apply only 2 to 3 inches of mulch on clay soils, somewhat deeper on well-drained sandy soils. This does not mean adding 2 to 3 inches yearly; not all of it will decompose in that time. Add only enough to maintain a total depth of 2 to 3 inches.

Vigorous overwatering may be a more common trigger of plant disease than the drought conditions gardeners seek to overcome. In waterlogged soils, root function suffers because oxygen levels are low. When oxygen is scarce, certain root-rotting fungi such as the aptly named water molds, *Pythium* and *Phytophthora,* flourish. And roots stressed by oxygen deprivation are more susceptible to infection by these pathogens. Watering properly involves keen observational skills. Check the soil to the depth of several inches; in most cases, if the soil is still moist, let it dry out, then water thoroughly.

Overfertilizing is another classic case of too much of a good thing.

Fertilizers provide important nutrients for the plant, but remember to use the recommended rates for each plant at the correct time of year. For example, pear trees given too much nitrogen rapidly put out shoots, and this succulent growth is more susceptible to fire blight. Many turfgrass diseases are more severe on overfertilized lawns. Roots can also suffer from overly high levels of fertilizer: they will lose water through osmosis when fertilizer salt concentrations are higher in the surrounding soil—this is how fertilizers "burn" roots.

Finally, be careful to prevent girdling when transplanting trees and shrubs. When woody plants are installed, the twine or wire holding the burlap in place often is not removed. Consequently, as the stem increases in girth over the years, the non-degradable twine or wire becomes ever tighter. Eventually it is imbedded inside of the bark in the plant's phloem, the pipeline that brings the products of photosynthesis down the stem to the roots. In the end, the roots will starve, and the stems and leaves will die from lack of water. All for want of removing that twine.

8. REMEMBER, DISEASE IS IN THE EYE OF THE BEHOLDER.

One of the most important things to keep in mind is that you don't have to prevent *all* of the myriad illnesses that could descend on your garden. You could prevent tar spot of maple with fungicides, but why bother? Maples do well year after year despite the disease. Lilacs are infected by powdery mildew year after year, but it never seems to hurt the plant; you probably couldn't kill your lilacs, even if you wanted to. There are many examples of such "harmless" diseases, from *Phyllosticta* leaf spot of maple, to many of the anthracnose diseases of ornamental plants. Some diseases you can—and should—learn to live with, and others you will want to concentrate on preventing.

9. FUNGICIDES ARE DISEASE PREVENTIVES.

Even when you do decide to use fungicides, prevention is still the key. All but a few fungicides must be applied before the fungus enters plant tissue to prevent infections and subsequent disease development. Timing is crucial: even with fungicides prevention—not cure—is the name of the game.

LEAST-TOXIC CONTROLS OF PLANT DISEASES

WILLIAM QUARLES

THE BEST WAY TO CONTROL PLANT DISEASES is to make sure they don't get a foothold in the garden in the first place. The preventive techniques described in "A Plant Disease Primer," starting on page 6—including applying compost, watering properly, carefully cleaning tools with a bleach solution, and planting resistant varieties—will help assure the health of your soil and plants. If a disease does get established, these same methods will also go a long way toward keeping it in check. Sometimes, though, when a particularly valuable plant is declining under the attack of a virulent pathogen or when weather conditions are especially conducive to a disease already established in your garden,

Bicarbonate, though nontoxic and effective against powdery mildew, may build to damaging levels in the soil, when used in conjunction with drip-type irrigation or in case of drought.

you may feel that it's necessary to resort to one of the controls described below.

Some of the least-toxic controls can be found in garden centers and hardware stores alongside a bewildering assortment of chemical pesticides. Others you can make yourself from ingredients that are often readily available. You will find recipes and information on when and how to apply these controls throughout this chapter. The Suppliers section on pages 102–103 lists the sources for many of the ingredients that are available commercially.

Success in disease suppression depends on matching plant, disease, and treatment. You will have to experiment to find the approach that's most effective. Be sure to test all of these formulations on a small area of a plant before committing valuable specimens to a full treatment. Although least-toxic pesticides are not perfect, their advantages outweigh possible disadvantages, making them good candidates for an integrated control program (see box on page 95). There are many different products to choose from, most of them readily available, and inexpensive. On the downside, some of the least-toxic controls have to be applied on a weekly basis, and they are not effective for all diseases. Specific problems that arise from repeated use can be avoided by rotating materials. Baking soda, for example, can give good control of powdery mildews, but overuse can tie up important soil minerals and lead to decreased plant growth. When this occurs, another material can be used instead.

Most of the controls mentioned in this chapter have low acute toxicity to mammals, including humans, and most are not toxic to beneficial insects. Some, such as baking soda, are practically non-toxic, while others, including bordeaux mixture, lime-sulfur, concentrated silicate salts, and streptomycin should be used with caution. Always follow application instructions carefully and apply only at the appropriate time in the plant's growth cycle and at the proper time of day. Be sure to protect yourself using the proper precautions when applying these controls. It is wise to avoid inhaling any kind of pesticide spray.

CONTROLLING FUNGAL DISEASES

Most garden diseases are caused by fungi: more than 8,000 species are known plant pathogens and either inhabit the aboveground portions of plants or are denizens of the soil. Most of the fungicides described below are essentially preventive measures, acting as barriers between pathogenic agents and plant tissues, and must be applied before new leaves or other susceptible plant parts appear, at the first sign of disease, or when weather conditions are favorable for disease.

FOLIAR FUNGICIDES

Copper and Sulfur

Sulfur, lime-sulfur, and bordeaux mixture—a combination of copper sulfate and lime—have been used as fungicides for a hundred years or more. These are all toxic to mammals, so avoid ingesting them and wear protective clothing when applying them. Bordeaux mixture is both fungicidal and bactericidal, and can be useful against diseases such as leaf spot and apple scab, among others. It contains copper sulfate, which is acidic, and lime, which is alkaline and helps neutralize the acidic salt. This mixture is a potent eye, skin, and gastrointestinal irritant and highly corrosive, and can cause nausea and vomiting if ingested. Bordeaux mixture can be applied as a dust or purchased in a liquid formulation, which is easier to use, especially if larger areas are involved.

LEAST-TOXIC CONTROL

BAKING SODA

Add 1 Tbsp. baking soda to a gallon of water. When the baking soda has dissolved, add ¼ to ½ tsp. of insecticidal or other liquid soap. Shake well.

DISEASES CONTROLLED
Powdery mildew; black spot

HOW OFTEN TO APPLY
Weekly

PRECAUTIONS
Detergent can cause plant damage; concentrations greater than 1 Tbsp./gallon may be toxic to roses; baking soda can accumulate in soil.

Sulfur can be used as a preventive fungicide against apple scab, brown rot, powdery mildew, rose black spot, rusts, and other diseases. You can apply sulfur as a dust or purchase it in liquid form; it is acidic and can irritate eyes and lungs. But do not use sulfur if you have applied an oil spray within the last month. Sulfur can injure plants if used when temperatures exceed 80°F. Lime is sometimes added to sulfur to help it penetrate plant tissue, but this mixture is more caustic than sulfur on its own and can cause severe eye and skin irritation. Do not inhale or ingest and wear protective clothing and eye-wear when applying.

Sprays Containing Salts

Baking Soda: Baking soda (sodium bicarbonate) is non-toxic, readily available, and very inexpensive. It can be effective against powdery mildew and somewhat useful against black spot. If you repeatedly spray leaves with bicarbonate, though, it will eventually reach the soil below, where it can accumulate and lead to slower plant growth. Bicarbonate can form insoluble particles with calcium and magnesium ions when it con-

LEAST-TOXIC CONTROL

PHOSPHATES

Add 1 Tbsp. of phosphate salt to a gallon of water containing about ¼ to ½ tsp. of liquid soap or detergent.

DISEASES CONTROLLED
Powdery mildew; rust; leaf blight

HOW OFTEN TO APPLY
Every 12–15 days

PRECAUTIONS
Spray small area first to check for plant damage. Wait at least two full days before treating the entire plant.

centrates in the soil, making these important nutrients unavailable to plants. High levels can also prevent plants from absorbing iron and can lead to chlorosis.

Bicarbonate is most likely to build to damaging levels in drought-stressed areas where there is little rain to flush it away. It is also likely to build up when applied in a small area, and when used in conjunction with drip-type irrigation. Garden situations are so complex that it is hard to predict the point at which you will see adverse effects. Stop applying bicarbonate sprays, however, at the first sign of plant damage or lower quality blooms.

Phosphate Salts: Foliar sprays containing potassium phosphate salts, unlike most of the non-toxic sprays, can not only prevent powdery mildew but in some instances even cure it. These salts seem to stimulate a systemic effect that builds up plant resistance to other diseases, including some forms of rust and northern leaf blight. Phosphate salts are ideal as foliar sprays because plants quickly absorb and circulate them. Other advantages are their low cost, low toxicity, and environmental safety (phosphate buffers, salt mixtures that protect against rapid changes in pH, are constructed from these salts and often used in soft drinks). Phosphate salts can even improve plant growth, as they may increase plant nutrition. Effects of added phosphate are most pronounced on plants deficient in phosphorus. Like any salt, though, these can damage plants when applied as foliar sprays. Test small areas before applying to whole plants. You can purchase phosphate salts from chemical supply houses and some horticultural nurseries. (Dibasic potassium phosphate is slightly less effective as a fungicide than the monobasic salt.)

Silica and Silicate Salts: Organic gardeners have long used sprays containing extracts of the common plant horsetail *(Equisetum arvense)* (which contains 15 to 40 percent natural silica) to protect against fungal diseases. Scientific experiments have recently verified this garden folklore, and show that potassium silicate solutions can protect cucumbers against damping-off, and cucumbers, grapes, and squash against powdery mildew. Sodium silicate can also protect plants against disease. How these salts act isn't clear yet, but like the phosphate salts above, they may be absorbed by plants and act systemically; such was the case with the cucumbers in the experiments above. Spray small areas to check for phytotoxicity before general use. Sodium or potassium silicate solutions can be obtained at drugstores. *Caution: be extremely careful when using silicate salts, as the concentrated solution is strongly alkaline.*

Oils

Petroleum-based horticultural oils (mineral oils), essential plant oils, neem oil, vegetable seed oils, and even fatty acids can be used effectively not just to fight insect pests, but to control pathogenic fungi as well. Oil sprays protect against fungi probably by helping to repel the water that is needed for fungal growth. The best approach to protection and control may be to rotate different classes of oil. Rotation of oils minimizes possible environmental accumulation of one kind. Petroleum is the most persistent; vegetable and neem oils are more easily biodegradable.

Petroleum-based oils: These oils have a long history of use in horticulture. Before the 1970s when lighter formulations were developed, orchardists sprayed their trees in the spring, while the trees were still dormant, with heavy ("dormant") oils to protect against insect pests. You can now purchase refined horticultural oils such as a product named Sun-Spray, which is effective against powdery mildew and sometimes against black spot. You can also purchase mineral oil at a drugstore and use it to make your own, less expensive, spray. Horticultural oils should not be used on drought-stressed plants or those weakened by disease, and they

LEAST-TOXIC CONTROL

SILICA

Dissolve ¼ tsp. of 30% potassium silicate in a gallon of water. Or: Boil ¼ cup of dried horsetail in 1 gallon of water for 20 minutes. Let liquid stand overnight. Filter through coffee filter or cheese cloth.

DISEASES CONTROLLED
Damping-off; powdery mildew

HOW OFTEN TO APPLY
Use as spray or, at least on cucumber, as a root drench (apply to base of plant, add water with hose until soil is soaked). Apply every 14 days.

PRECAUTIONS
Handle silica salts with extreme care, as the concentrated solution is strongly alkaline. Spray small area to check for plant damage. Wait at least two days before treating entire plant.

LEAST-TOXIC CONTROL

VEGETABLE OILS

Add 3 Tbsp. of oil to 1 gallon of water containing ¼ to ½ tsp. of liquid soap or detergent.

DISEASES CONTROLLED
Powdery mildew

HOW OFTEN TO APPLY
Every 7–14 days

PRECAUTIONS
Spray small area first to check for plant damage.

LEAST-TOXIC CONTROL

MINERAL OIL SOLUTION

Add ½ tsp. of liquid soap or detergent to a pint of mineral oil to make a concentrate. Add 3 Tbsp. of this concentrate to 1 gallon of water to make a 1% solution.

DISEASES CONTROLLED
Powdery mildew

HOW OFTEN TO APPLY
Every 7–14 days

PRECAUTIONS
Spray small area first to check for plant damage.

should not be used when temperatures exceed 85°F. With repeated use petroleum-based sprays can also build up in your soil.

Vegetable oil sprays: Cooking and salad oils are more readily available than most other oils and are probably less disruptive to the environment. Vegetable oils are biodegradable and shouldn't cause any long-term problems in the garden. Emulsified vegetable oil sprays of sunflower, olive, canola, peanut, soybean, corn, grapeseed, or safflower can control powdery mildew on apple trees, roses, and possibly other plants, and cottonseed oil has considerable protective value against powdery mildew. However, emulsified vegetable oil can leave a greasy film on leaves, which you might find objectionable. Check for plant damage before general use, and be especially careful of blooms.

Herbal oil sprays: Essential oils such as those made from basil, fenugreek, cumin, mint, clove, and eucalyptus may be effective against a number of fungal pathogens. For instance, solutions of cumin or clove oil completely inhibit sugarcane rot, and basil oil can inhibit growth of soilborne pathogens. A commercial formulation of mint oil (Funga-Stop) is available to help control soilborne pathogens. However, these essential oils need to be researched further before they become prevalent in horticulture.

Neem oil: Neem is derived from the neem tree, a native of Myanmar (the former Burma) and

COMBINATION TREATMENTS

YOU MAY HAVE GREATER SUCCESS combating plant diseases when you combine control treatments instead of employing a single control strategy. For example, baking soda is usually more effective when used with oil because both have antifungal properties. The oil may also help provide an even distribution of baking soda on plant leaves.

Pathogens can also develop resistance to ingredients that are applied frequently, so a rotation of active ingredients can reduce the likelihood of pathogen resistance. Combination treatments can be applied simultaneously or sequentially, in a planned rotation. There are so many complex interactions taking place in each home garden that you will have to come up with the most effective treatment rotations through trial and error. A good rule might be to start experimenting with the least expensive and most readily available products first. To control fungal diseases, for example, it's likely that you will have to spray weekly, especially in areas of high rainfall; so this time interval might be a good starting point to set a rotation schedule. Adjust the schedule through trial and error. You might get away with fewer applications, or you might need more frequent treatments.

Some examples of treatment rotations:

1. To prevent powdery mildew, rotate vinegar, baking soda, and vegetable oil (the least expensive and most easily available remedies). Spray plants once a week, alternating substances.

2. Black spot and rust require preventive sprays. Neem oil sprays in rotation with antitranspirants or garlic might prevent these diseases, especially on resistant species. The systemic effect of phosphate salts could be useful as well.

3. Antitranspirants can protect against mildew for up to 30 days. Foliage put out in that interval, however, is not protected. You can protect it by spraying with baking soda or another foliar spray between applications of antitranspirants.

As diseases and severity vary with location, you will have to experiment to find the most effective combination. With all these options, there is no longer any need to use toxic sprays, especially when resistant species and good cultural practices can help prevent the problem in the first place.

LEAST-TOXIC CONTROL

NEEM OIL

Use 2½ Tbsp. per gallon of water. Shake well.

DISEASES CONTROLLED
Powdery mildew, rust, *Botrytis* gray mold, downy mildew

HOW OFTEN TO APPLY
Every 7–14 days

PRECAUTIONS
Spray small area first to check for plant damage.

LEAST-TOXIC CONTROL

SOAPS

Add 2½ Tbsp. of liquid soap to a gallon of water. Shake well.

DISEASES CONTROLLED
Powdery mildew

HOW OFTEN TO APPLY
Every 7–14 days

PRECAUTIONS
Spray small area first to check for plant damage.

India. Extracts of neem seeds are used as insecticides; they kill insects as they molt or hatch. Recently, fungicides made with neem oil have become available commercially. Neem oil appears to have better fungicidal properties than many of the oils described above, perhaps because neem contains sulfur compounds, which have their own fungicidal properties, as well as other natural pesticides. A neem-oil formulation called Trilogy has been approved by the EPA for use on foods, while Rose Defense and Triact (for control of powdery mildew, rust, black spot, *Botrytis*, downy mildew, and other common diseases) are designed for use on ornamentals. Make sure you buy neem with fungicidal rather than insecticidal properties.

Soaps

Like many other methods outlined here, soaps have been used for many years by organic gardeners, particularly as insecticides. Commercial formulations now include soap solutions with fungicidal properties, which show some control of powdery mildew, black spot, canker, leaf spot, and rust. You can also make your own version. All soaps can damage plants when applied improperly. Test before you spray widely.

Botanicals

Plant preparations have been used for centuries in medicine and pest control. For example, opium from the opium poppy was one of the first pain killers. Farmers in India use neem leaves to protect their stored grain from insects. Herbs and spices, such as basil and clove, have been used by many cultures to protect food from spoilage, as both have antimicrobial properties.

Milsana: The German corporation BASF capitalized on this concept in 1993 by screening a large number of plant extracts for their fungicidal properties. The most promising result was a dried extract of the giant knotweed, *Reynoutria sachalinensis,* which is now sold as a fungicide under the brandname Milsana. Knotweed extract has only recently become commercially available in the United States, so feedback from

CONTROLLING SOILBORNE PATHOGENS

CONVENTIONALLY, SOILBORNE PATHOGENS are controlled by soil fumigation or by addition of chemical fungicides to the soil. The most commonly used soil fumigant is methyl bromide, a toxic and dangerous gas that also depletes the stratospheric ozone layer. Another common soil fungicide is Dazomet (sold under the brand name Basamid), a granular material that releases a toxic gas when it comes in contact with the water in the soil. Among the alternatives to these poisons are plants such as garlic that release fungicidal chemicals into the soil. Rotation of garlic with tomatoes, for instance, can reduce the likelihood of soilborne tomato diseases. Incorporating broccoli residues into the soil can help disinfect your soil of the fungus that causes *Verticillium* wilt. In areas with abundant sunlight, you can solarize the soil to disinfect it of fungi, bacteria, nematodes, and even weed seeds (*see* page 83).

Seeds and soil can also be treated with biocontrol agents that prevent soilborne diseases (*see* "Antagonists," page 100). These beneficial bacteria and fungi work by competing with disease-causing organisms for nutrients and space, by producing antibiotics, by preying on pathogens, or by inducing resistance in the host plants. Biocontrol agents can help control damping-off, wilt, and a number of soilborne diseases caused by *Pythium, Fusarium, Rhizoctonia, Verticillium,* and other pathogens. Commercially available agents include the beneficial fungi *Trichoderma harzianum* (sold as Root Shield) and *Gliocladium virens* (SoilGard), and bacteria such as *Bacillus subtilis* (Kodiak), *Streptomyces griseoviridis* (Mycostop), and *Burkholderia cepacia* (Deny). These agents are non-toxic and some occur naturally in compost—but like compost, these agents are not always 100-percent effective at disease control.

For tips on controlling soilborne nematodes, see page 99.

LEAST-TOXIC CONTROL

GARLIC

Homogenize 2 bulbs of garlic (about ¼ lb) for 5–10 minutes in a blender with a quart of water containing a few drops of liquid soap. Filter through cheesecloth; refrigerate liquid. Label clearly.

DISEASES CONTROLLED
Mildew, rusts, fruit rots, blights, and black spot. Use full-strength for serious problems; dilute 1 part garlic stock in 9 parts water to prevent powdery mildew.

HOW OFTEN TO APPLY
Every 7–14 days

PRECAUTIONS
Spray small area first to check for plant damage.

U.S. gardeners is sparse. Italian researchers have found that Milsana reduced powdery mildew infection on cucumber by 50 percent, and similar sprays protected roses, but these were less effective than oils, soaps, and other non-toxic products. Repeated sprays of Milsana induced a greener and glossier coloration of the leaves, but they became brittle to the touch.

Garlic: Sprays made from aqueous garlic extracts have antibiotic and antifungal properties and will suppress a number of plant diseases, including powdery mildew on cucumbers and, to some extent, black spot on roses. Activity may be due to sulfur-containing compounds such as ajoene or allicin.

Antitranspirants
Antitranspirant coatings made from very dilute mixtures of polymers and water are sometimes sprayed onto foliage to prevent water loss. Growers also use them to protect a number of different ornamental plants against diseases caused by fungi. Antitranspirants are just as effective as some chemical fungicides against downy mildew on zinnia, hydrangea, and crapemyrtle, and against powdery mildew and black spot on roses. They are available commercially under the names Wilt-Pruf and Vapor Gard, among others.

Antitranspirant coatings are non-toxic, biodegradable, and inexpensive, and are readily available at local nurseries in liquid form. Unlike fungicides, their action against pathogens is non-specific and so they are not likely to cause a buildup of resistance. Antitranspirants do not protect new growth, though, so the coatings have to be reapplied on a regular basis. Since leaf coatings reduce the rate of photosynthesis by about 5 percent, antitranspirants are probably better suited for sunny climates.

CONTROLLING BACTERIAL DISEASES

There are very few effective chemical controls for bacterial diseases. Bordeaux mixture is one possible treatment for bacterial diseases occurring on stems and leaves. The active component in this mixture is copper ion, which is both fungicidal and bactericidal; it is commonly used for bacterial leaf spot. Some bacterial diseases, such as fire blight, walnut blight, and bacterial spot of tomato, can be treated with antibiotics, including streptomycin (sold as Agrimycin). *Caution: Agrimycin can be extremely toxic to mammals, aquatic invertebrates, fish, bees, and beneficial insects, and can cause plant damage.*

LEAST-TOXIC CONTROL

ANTITRANSPIRANTS

For a 3% by volume solution: add 7⅔ Tbsp. to a gallon of water. For a 4% by volume solution: use 10 Tbsp./gal.

DISEASES CONTROLLED
Powdery mildew, black spot, rust, some blights. For powdery mildew, use at 3%. For black spot, use at 4%.

HOW OFTEN TO APPLY
Every 10–30 days

PRECAUTIONS
Spray small area first to check for plant damage.

CONTROLLING VIRUSES

The most effective approach to viral diseases is to control the insect vectors that often transmit them from plant to plant. For instance, successful management of thrips can help prevent the spread of tomato spotted wilt virus. Non-toxic treatments are ineffective against viruses, and in response to chemical controls, viruses easily mutate. (See *Natural Insect Control: The Ecological Gardener's Guide to Foiling Pests,* 1994, Brooklyn Botanic Garden Handbook #139, for garden-safe methods for controlling insect pests.)

CONTROLLING NEMATODES

Parasitic nematodes are most often soilborne. Their effects can be minimized by rotating crops, increasing organic matter in the soil, and planting nematode-free material. Applying compost helps control nematodes because compost teems with bacteria and fungi that attack pathogens. Adding organic matter to the soil also helps create a large microbial soil population, and as these microbes feed near plant roots they form a barrier that makes nematode penetration less likely. If the problem is severe, you can combine compost and inoculations of plant roots with mycor-

An immature (larval) western flower thrip. Successful management of thrips can help prevent the spread of tomato spotted wilt virus. In general, controlling insect vectors is the most effective approach to viral diseases, which are most often transmitted by feeding insects.

rhizae, symbiotic fungi that help feed the plant by enhancing mineral uptake. Since mycorrhizae colonize roots, they make nematode penetration more difficult. You can also add beneficial nematodes, which can displace parasitic species.

You can add chitin—a polysaccharide complex found in both shellfish shells and nematode eggs—to the soil to help control nematodes; a commercial form called ClandoSan is available. This soil amendment stimulates the growth of soil microbes that produce chitinase, an enzyme that breaks down the chitin in nematode eggs, destroying the eggs and larvae. As chitin is metabolized, ammonia is released, which is toxic to nematodes.

ANTAGONISTS

Beneficial fungi or bacteria can control garden diseases by competing with disease-causing organisms for nutrients and space, by producing antibiotics, by preying on pathogens (a process called hyperparasitism), or by inducing resistance in the host plant. Antagonists do not persist in the environment, are non-toxic, and in some cases are as effective as chemical fungicides.

Beneficial fungi are effective only when humidity is high (usually 60 to 80 percent), so their usefulness is restricted to greenhouses or to regions, such as Louisiana and other Gulf states, where humidity is always very high during the summer growing season. Beneficial bacteria are less sensitive to moisture, and so have a wider range of use.

COMPETITION

Preliminary research shows that the beneficial bacterium *Bacillus laterosporus* (sold as Rose Flora) is as effective at protecting black spot-susceptible rose cultivars as some chemical fungicides. It probably protects against black spot through competition, but this agent is still relatively new and experiments detailing its mode of action have not been completed. As a ground spray, it can help control new sources of black spot infection. As a foliar spray, it seems to be more effective when mixed with the antitranspirant sold commercially as Wilt-Pruf. The powdered formulation can cause eye irritation, so use eye protection when mixing solutions and applying.

LEAST-TOXIC CONTROL

COMPOST TEA

Mix 1 part finished compost with 6 parts of water; let the mixture soak for a week. Filter off solids with cheesecloth. Dilute liquid until it has a tea-like color.

DISEASES CONTROLLED
Powdery mildew, *Botrytis* gray mold

HOW OFTEN TO APPLY
Every 14 days

PRECAUTIONS
Spray small area first to check for plant damage. Repeat with each new batch.

HYPERPARASITES

Ampelomyces quisqualis is a powdery mildew hyperparasite first described in the mid-nineteenth century. The fungus attacks a wide range of powdery mildew species and genera; it spreads naturally through the air, and acts quickly. The commercially available strain, AQ-10, can provide some control of powdery mildew on cucumber, grapes, roses, and possibly other plants. Research has shown that better results are obtained when AQ-10 is mixed with a horticultural-oil solution before spraying.

COMPOST TEA

Water extracts of fermented compost, or "compost teas," are full of antibiotics, microbial products, and beneficial microbes that compete with pathogens, such as those that are responsible for powdery mildew, *Botrytis* gray mold, and leaf blight. The "tea" can be used as a foliar spray to help suppress plant disease. Undiluted compost may also benefit a plant's roots, and stem, as well as the soil when applied as a thin layer of mulch around the plant.

SUPPLIERS

AGBIO DEVELOPMENT
9915 Raleigh St.
Westminister, CO 80031
877-268-2020
(soilborne biocontrol: *Streptomyces griseoviridis*—Mycostop; mycorrhizal inoculants)

BETTER FLORA
603 N. Kimball
Excelsior Springs, MO 64024
800-583-1939, 816-630-3399
www.better-flora.com
(biocontrol: *Bacillus laterosporus*—Rose Flora)

BIOLOGIC
P.O. Box 177
Willow Hill, PA 17271
717-349-2789
(beneficial nematodes)

BIOWORKS
122 N. Genesee St.
Geneva, NY 14456
800-877-9443
(soilborne biocontrol: *Trichoderma harzianum*—Root Shield)

ECOGEN INC.
2000 Cabot Blvd. West
Langhorne, PA 19047
800-220-2135, 215-757-1590
215-757-2956 fax
(biocontrol: *Ampelomyces quisqualis*—AQ-10)

GREENLIGHT COMPANY
P.O. Box 17985
San Antonio, TX 78217
800-777-5702, 210-494-3481
210-494-5224 fax
(neem oil: Rose Defense)

GUSTAFSON
P.O. Box 660065
Dallas, TX 75266
800-248-6907
(soilborne biocontrol: *Bacillus subtilis*—Kodiak)

HARMONY FARM SUPPLY
3244 Gravenstein Hwy. N.
Sebastopol, CA 95472
707-823-9125
707-823-1734 fax
(soilborne biocontrol: SoilGard)

JMS FLOWER FARMS
1105 25th Avenue
Vero Beach, FL 32960
561-567-9241
561-567-9394 fax
(horticultural oil: JMS Stylet Oil)

KHH BIOSCI. INC.
Centennial Campus Venture II Bldg.
920 Main Campus Drive, Suite 400
Raleigh, NC 27606
919-424-3737, ext. 350
919-424-3738 fax
(botanicals: giant knotweed—Milsana)

MARKET VI
6613 Haskins
Shawnee, KS 66216
913-268-7504
913-268-2694 fax
(soilborne biocontrol: Deny)

MILLER CHEMICAL AND FERTILIZER CO.
P.O. Box 333
Hanover, PA 17331
800-233-2040
(antitranspirant: Vapor Gard)

OLYMPIC HORTICULTURAL PRODUCTS
P.O. Box 1885
Bradenton, FL 34206
800-659-6745
888-647-4329 fax
www.hortnet.com/olympic
(neem oil: Triact)

PEACEFUL VALLEY
P.O. Box 2209
Grass Valley, CA 95945
888-784-1722
www.groworganic.com
(bactericides: streptomycin—
Agrimycin)

PERMAGUARD
115 Rio Bravo SE
Albuquerque, NM 87105
505-873-3061
505-873-3261 fax
(silica: food-grade diatomaceous earth)

PLANT HEALTH CARE
440 William Pitt Way
Pittsburgh, PA 15238
800-421-9051
(soilborne biocontrol: VAM
Mycorrhizae)

SOIL TECHNOLOGIES
2103 185th St.
Fairfield, IA 52556
800-221-7645, 515-472-3963
515-472-6189 fax
www.americanatural.com
(mint oil: Funga-Stop)

STOLLER ENTERPRISES
8580 Katy Freeway, Suite 200
Houston, TX 77024
800-539-5283, 713-464-5580
713-461-4467 fax
(hormone products)

SUN OIL
1801 Market St.
Philadelphia, PA 19103
800-345-1142
(horticultural oil: SunSpray)

VERDANT BRANDS INC.
9555 James Ave. South, Suite 200
Bloomington, MN 55431
800-423-7544, 612-703-3300
612-887-1300 fax
www.verdantbrands.com
(insecticidal soap: Safer; Bordeaux
mixture)

WILT-PRUF PRODUCTS
P.O. Box 469
Essex, CT 06426
800-972-0726, 860-767-7033
860-767-7265 fax
(antitranspirant: Wilt-Pruf)

For more listings see the *2000
Directory of Least-Toxic Pest Control,*
Bio-Integral Resource Center,
P.O. Box 7414, Berkeley, CA 94707
510-524-2567, 510-524-1758 fax,
birc@igc.org; www.birc.org

FOR MORE INFORMATION

**DISEASES AND PESTS OF
ORNAMENTAL PLANTS, 5TH EDITION**
Pascal P. Pirone
John Wiley & Sons, 1978

**THE GARDENER'S GUIDE TO PLANT
DISEASES: EARTH-SAFE REMEDIES**
Barbara Pleasant
Storey Communications, 1995

**THE ORGANIC GARDENER'S
HANDBOOK OF NATURAL INSECT
AND DISEASE CONTROL**
Edited by Barbara Ellis and Fern
Marshall Bradley
Rodale Press, 1992

**RODALE'S GARDEN INSECT, DISEASE,
& WEED IDENTIFICATION GUIDE**
Miranda Smith and Anna Carr
Rodale Press, 1988

**RODALE'S PEST AND DISEASE
PROBLEM SOLVER**
Linda Gilkeson, Pam Peirce, and
Miranda Smith
Rodale Press, 1996

**WESTCOTT'S PLANT DISEASE
HANDBOOK, 5TH EDITION**
revised by R. Kenneth Horst
Van Nostrand Reinhold, 1990

WORLD WIDE WEB
The American Phytopathological
Society maintains a web site
(http://www.scisoc.org/) that
includes a directory of Extension
plant pathologists in every state and
some good general information on
plant disease. At this site you can
also link to universities with plant
pathology departments; these sites
often contain plant-disease information relevant to gardeners in their
region.

Right: Gymnosporangium rust gall
with spore horns on cedar.

CONTRIBUTORS

JIM CHATFIELD is an assistant professor and Extension specialist with the Ohio State University Extension, where he has worked for the past 12 years. He teaches and writes extensively on plant pathology, plant selection, and plant diagnostic topics.

MARGERY DAUGHTREY is a senior Extension associate with the Department of Plant Pathology at Cornell University and is stationed at Cornell's Long Island Horticultural Research and Extension Center in Riverhead, New York. She has conducted a research and Extension program on the management of diseases of ornamental plants for the past 22 years.

PATRICIA DONALD is a research assistant professor with the Department of Plant Microbiology and Pathology at the University of Missouri and is the director of the Extension Nematology Laboratory at the university. She specializes in the management of plant parasitic nematodes.

ETHEL DUTKY has been director of the Plant Diagnostic Laboratory for the Maryland Cooperative Extension Service since 1979. She is coauthor of *Pests and Diseases of Herbaceous Perennials*, published by Ball Press in 1999.

WADE H. ELMER is a plant pathologist at the Connecticut Agricultural Experiment Station in New Haven. His interests include soilborne fungal pathogens of vegetables, small fruits, and ornamentals.

BETH HANSON is former managing editor of Brooklyn Botanic Garden's 21st Century Gardening Series. She guest-edited the 1997 handbook *Easy Compost* and the 2000 handbook *Chile Peppers*, and contributed to *The Brooklyn Botanic Garden Gardener's Desk Reference* (Henry Holt, 1998).

STEPHEN T. NAMETH is an associate professor in the Department of Plant Pathology at Ohio State University. His research centers on the identification and control of viruses and virus-induced diseases of ornamental plants.

MELODIE PUTNAM is the diagnostic plant pathologist and Extension educator in the Botany and Plant Pathology Department at Oregon State University, and has been diagnosing plant problems since 1981. She is also the director of the OSU Plant Clinic.

WILLIAM QUARLES is an integrated pest management (IPM) specialist and the executive director of the Bio-Integral Resource Center (BIRC) in Berkeley, California, a non-profit organization that researches pesticide alternatives and educates the public about them.

MIRANDA SMITH has been teaching organic agriculture since 1971, and has worked in many regions of the U.S. and several provinces in Canada. She is author or co-author of 11 books about horticulture, including *Rodale's Pest And Disease Problem Solver: A Chemical-Free Guide to Keeping Your Garden Healthy*.

KAREN L. SNOVER is the director of the Plant Disease Diagnostic Clinic of the Department of Plant Pathology at Cornell University. She diagnoses plant diseases on a wide range of host plants, such as woody ornamentals, herbaceous plants, fruits, vegetables, turfgrass, and field crops.

ILLUSTRATIONS AND PHOTOS

All illustrations by **STEVE BUCHANAN**

ETHEL DUTKY cover, pages 27 left, 35, 40, 64

DAVID CAVAGNARO pages 1, 5, 8 top left, 10, 15, 16 bottom left, 24, 31, 47, 51, 55, 56, 57, 60, 77

ROBERT P. MULROONEY/UNIVERSITY OF DELAWARE, pages 7, 8 bottom right, 29, 30 left, 36 left and right, 38, 42, 49, 52 bottom, 53, 61, 65 left, 68, 71 right, 73, 75 left and right

ANNE BIRD SINDERMANN/MARYLAND DEPARTMENT OF AGRICULTURE pages 8 top right, 25, 26, 32, 34

ALAN & LINDA DETRICK pages 8 bottom left, 11 bottom, 12, 16 top left and right, bottom right, 27 right, 37, 46, 58, 63, 70

AMERICAN PHYTOPATHOLOGICAL SOCIETY pages 11 top, 30 right, 33, 44, 65 right, 71 left, 100, 104

STEPHEN T. NAMETH pages 28, 41, 43

R. KENNETH HORST page 39

ANITA SABARESE pages 48, 52 top

LEE A. REICH pages 50, 89

WADE H. ELMER pages 59, 62

PATRICIA S. MICHALAK page 72

ELVIN McDONALD page 78

INDEX

Oil sprays, as fungicide, 93-96
Olive-green spots, causes of, 17
Onion, 22
Orange strings, 17
Ornamental plants, diseases, 19, 24-44

P
Pachysandra, 19
Parsnip, 22
Pea, 22
Peach, 21
Peach leaf curl, 17, 20, 21, 51-52
Pear, 21, 88
Pear scab, 21, 45-46
Peony, leaf spot of, 17, 19, 35-36
Pepper, 22
Perennials, diseases of, 19, 24-44
Peronospora, 32
Petroleum oils, as fungicide, 93-94
Phlox, 19
Phosphate salts, as fungicide, 92
Photinia, 20
Phragmidium, 40
Phyllosticta leaf spot of Maple, 20, 52-53, 88
Phytophthora
  and flooding injury, 71
  infestans, 59
  root rot, 17, 18, 20, 22, 36-37, 87
Phytoplasma, 25
Pine, 21
  Diplodia tip blight of, 21, 47-48
  salt injury, 79
  White Pine blister rust, 17, 18, 20, 54
Planting depth, 84
Plum, 21

Poplar, 21
Potato, 22, 59, 60
  late blight of, 80-81
Powdery mildews, 8, 9
  about, 37-38
  as "harmless", 88
  plants affected by, 19, 20, 21, 22, 53, 60
  prevention and control of, 91-96, 98, 99, 101
  symptoms, 17, 18
Privet, 20
Pruning, 82, 85, 86
Pseudoperonospora, 32
Pumpkin, 22
Pyracantha, 20
Pythium
  and damping-off, 31
  and flooding injury, 71
  root rot, 9, 17, 19, 21, 38-39, 61, 87

Q
Quince, 20

R
Ralstonia solanacearum, 56
Red thread, 18, 22, 64-65
Resistant plants, 7, 79-80
Rhizoctonia solani, 31
Rhizoctonia zeae, 63
Rhododendron, 20
Rhytisma, 53-54
Roguing, 81
Root-knot nematodes, 17, 18, 19, 20, 21, 61
Root rots
  black, 17, 18, 19, 20, 26-27, 78
  and mulching, 87
  Phytophthora, 17, 18, 20, 22, 36-37, 87

Pythium, 9, 17, 19, 21, 38-39, 61, 87
  and watering, 85
Root symptoms, 18
Rose, 20
  black spot of, 20, 27-28, 80, 81, 101
  rust, 17, 20, 39-40
Rots, 9, 11
  blossom end rot, 11
  See also Root rots
Rudbeckia, 19
Rusts
  Gymnosporangium, 12, 17, 18, 20, 21, 51
  prevention of, 95, 96, 99
  Rose, 17, 20, 39-40
  symptoms of, 17
  turfgrass, 22, 65-66
  White Pine blister, 17, 18, 20, 54
Ryegrass, 22

S
Salt injury, 17, 18, 74-75, 79
Sanitation practices, 80-82
Scab, Apple, 17, 18, 20, 21, 45-46, 76-77, 80
Sclerospora, 32
Sclerotinia, 43
Sclerotium rolfsii, 42
Seedlings, damping off, 17, 30-31, 57
Septoria blight, 17, 19, 20, 21, 22, 40-41 53, 61
Shoot/tip blights on Junipers, 18, 21, 41, 53
Shrubs
  disease prevention, 85, 86-87, 88
  diseases of, 20
  planting depth, 84

BROOKLYN BOTANIC GARDEN

MORE

BOOKS ON

GARDENING

TECHNIQUES

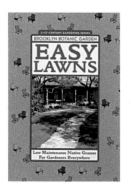